Disney
TSUM TSUM
Sushi Cookbook

BY EMI TSUNEOKA

VIZ MEDIA

CONTENTS

How to Use This Book

▶ The difficulty of each sushi roll is represented by the number of ♥. The level of difficulty is ♥ → ♥♥ → ♥♥♥, and the more hearts there are, the more difficult it is.

▶ The photograph below the title of each roll is close to its actual size. Please use it as a reference when you are making the sushi. However, nori does shrink a little after some time, so there will be some differences with the completed product.

▶ The amounts used in the recipe are 1 cup = 200 ml, 1 teaspoon = 5 ml, 1 tablespoon = 15 ml.

Pro Tip
We have listed measurements in both grams and ounces for convenience. But it will be most accurate to use a digital scale that can swap between different measurement settings.

GATHER AROUND, TSUM TSUM SUSHI ROLLS!

Okay, it's time for Tsum Tsum sushi roll party! Create your favorite Tsum Tsum character rolls and stack them up however you like!

STACK MICKEY AND HIS FRIENDS IN A PYRAMID SHAPE

Mickey, Minnie, Donald, Daisy, Pluto, and Goofy. Stack your favorite classic Disney characters into a colorful mountain. The ears and hands fit perfectly into the triangular shape.

4

FUN WITH THE TSUM TSUMS

Stitch, Baymax (red), Little Green Men, Mike, and Perry. Cheerful Tsum Tsums with unique colors and shapes. Stack them as if they are moving around!

CHARMING TSUM TSUMS

Cinderella, Snow White, Tinker Bell, Anna, and Elsa. You'll be enchanted by their beautiful hair, cute expressions, and lovely round eyes.

CHARACTERS WITH CUTE RIBBONS

Minnie, Daisy, and Marie. Minnie has a red polka-dotted ribbon, Daisy and Marie are wearing pink ribbons. Who's the cutest?!

WHITE TSUM TSUMS

Donald, Daisy, Marie, Olaf, and Baymax. Tsum Tsums with characters whose base color is white. The colors of their nose, beak and ribbon will stand out very nicely.

BLUE TSUM TSUMS

Stitch, Sulley, and Perry. Stack the blue characters in a triangle. Round-faced Sulley is being supported by mischievous Stitch and Perry.

GREEN TSUM TSUMS

Little Green Men, Mike, and Peas-in-a-Pod. The green characters are a unique bunch with lots of eyes. They always give off a happy and cheerful vibe.

Tsum Tsum Sushi Roll Q&A

"I can't roll the sushi roll well!"
"I'm having trouble! What are the tricks?"
We'll answer all your questions!

Q I'm a very slow roller.

A The preparation will make a huge difference!

The most important thing is to prepare to perfection. Arrange all the tools you need before you, cut the nori sheets to size → weigh the vinegared rice precisely → prepare the small decorations. If you remember to do all that preparation beforehand, you should be able to smoothly get through the rolling process.

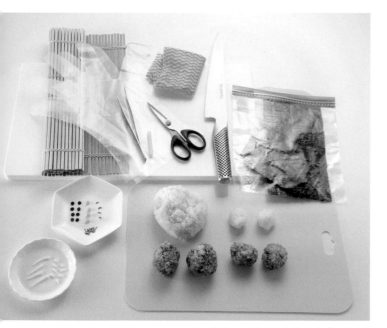

Set everything up before starting to roll.

Q The vinegared rice and nori keep sticking to my hands.

A Use embossed plastic gloves.

One reason the rolling feels like it is taking a long time is because the rice and nori keep sticking to your hand. The rice will stick more easily if your hands are dry, so the basic rule is to keep your hands wet with vinegar water. But for people who are not used to it, we strongly advise you use embossed plastic gloves. It will make working with the vinegared rice and nori a lot easier.

Use embossed plastic gloves.

Q The nori starts to get damp when I'm rolling the sushi.

A Your sushi mat could be wet.

Be careful not to wet your sushi mat while working. If you happen to get it wet during the rolling, use a paper towel to wipe it off. The best method is to use a dry towel to wipe off any rice and nori fragments that have clung onto the mat after every roll you make. After each use, wash the sushi mat clean to remove any rice and let it fully air dry.

Q It's very difficult to cut the cheese slices freehand.

A Create a simple template with parchment paper.

It may be difficult to cut out intricate patterns with a bamboo skewer at first. The photograph of the final sushi roll in this recipe book is very close to its actual size, so trace the outlines of the pieces with pencil or something on parchment paper, cut it out and use that as a template. Place the template on the cheese and trace along the edges with a bamboo skewer, and you should be able to cut it in the shape you want.

Trace over the piece you need from the photographs of the recipe.

Cut the baking paper, place it on the cheese and cut along its edge.

Q Things move a lot when I roll them!

A Make sure to check as you go.

There can be several reasons the various parts you've assembled and are trying to roll start to move out of place. Firstly, you may have placed it in the wrong place to begin with. And secondly, the parts and smaller rolls may be shifting out of place as you roll them into the larger roll. So remember to check from the front of the roll if the design looks correct every time you add a new piece and fix it if it doesn't. Don't forget to do a final check at the very end before rolling the sushi roll.

Hold them up at eye level to check if they look right.

Q Why doesn't the final roll look nice?

A The rice needs to be very precisely weighed so it spreads evenly.

At times you will have trouble creating a nice-looking sushi roll because you did not have enough rice or failed to even out the rice on the nori sheet. When you spread the rice out, make sure it has been spread out exactly where it should be and check if there are any places that need more rice. If you notice a lack of rice somewhere, pick up some rice from areas with too much rice and move it. When moving the rice, you will get better results if you shape the rice into the size and shape of the area that needs more rice.

Place onto the nori after the rice has been spread out into a stick shape that is 4 inches / 10 cm long.

Use a bamboo skewer to create a hole where the body part needs to be attached. Attach thin pasta (uncooked) to the body part and then pin that body part to the roll. The pasta will absorb the moisture after a while and will naturally soften, so they are edible.

Q What should I pay attention to when placing the roll in a lunch box?

A Firmly connect any pieces that may easily fall apart.

When you're packing a lunch with Tsum Tsum sushi rolls, it is best to choose characters that don't have pieces like ears, ribbons, and hats that need to be attached at the end. But we know you want to include cute Mickey and Minnie in the lunch box too! If you want to do that, our advice is to connect those parts to the roll using edible ingredients. And pack the box tightly with other side dishes, so the sushi roll will not move around in the box.

Use the palm of your hand to spread the rice evenly so it will cover the area the rice needs to be placed on.

Q Any ideas for using the sushi rolls as a little present?

A They look even cuter if you wrap them!

Even a single slice will look like a nice gift if you wrap it cutely. Transparent plastic bags are easy to use because you can see the decorations on the roll inside it. Don't forget to connect the smaller parts onto the roll using the technique for packing a lunch when placing the sushi rolls in the bag.

Open the bag, place the sushi roll in a cupcake wrapper, and push it into the bag using chopsticks.

Close the bag using cute ribbons and tape.

Stack them up like Tsum Tsum when placing them in a gift box.

Tsum Tsum Sushi Basics & Tips

TOOLS

Here are the tools you need to make Tsum Tsum sushi rolls. It's a good idea to prepare these before you start.

The basic three tools for vinegared rice

Bowls, rice paddle, fan

Mix the hot rice and sushi vinegar in a large bowl and fan it to create vinegared rice. It is also convenient to prepare several smaller bowls to make the colored vinegared rice.

A must-have for the sushi roll

Sushi mat

Bamboo sushi mats for thick sushi rolls are the most basic tool. Make sure they are dry when you use them with the slightly green side facing up and the knots on the far side. Colored plastic sushi mats that can be dried just by wiping them are useful too.

Deco Sushi Mat provided by Clover

Cutting board

A large plastic chopping board is hygienic and easy to use. It will be useful if you have a chopping board with a ruler on it to measure the length and width of the ingredients and vinegared rice. If not, you can use an 8 inch / 20 cm ruler.

Scale

You will need this to weigh the ingredients precisely. The ingredients of Tsum Tsum sushi rolls are in small measurements of 0.18 oz / 5 g and 0.35 oz / 10 g, so it will be useful to have a scale that can weigh down to the decimals.

Measuring cup, spoons

Used to measure volumes.
1 cup = 200 ml
1 tablespoon = 15 ml
1 teaspoon = 5 ml

Recommended!

Embossed plastic gloves

These are disposable plastic gloves. The vinegared rice won't stick to your fingers, so wearing them will help you with the work that needs precision.

Kitchen knife

Long and thin-bladed kitchen knives are the best for sushi rolls. A chef's knife or a paring knife with a slightly long blade will do.

Kitchen shears

These are very useful to cut the nori sheets. We recommend using kitchen scissors with a sharp tip for cutting the thin strands of nori for the eyelashes.

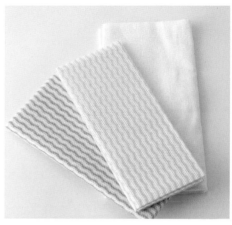

Kitchen towel

Used for various purposes, such as wiping your hands, kitchen knife and tools, as well as placing it over the vinegared rice to avoid the rice and ingredients from drying. Non-woven towels are the best to wipe off the rice that is stuck to the kitchen knife.

Nori sheet puncher

Hole punches that can be used to punch out eyebrows, eyes, noses and mouths from the nori sheets. You can use scissors if you don't have one.

To cut out parts for the eyes and noses.

Straw

Prepare various sizes to cut circles, ovals, and triangles out of thick ingredients (soy sauce kelp and fish sausage) that are too thick for the nori sheet puncher. (Read "Preparing the small pieces" on page 25 for the details.)

Tweezers, bamboo skewer, chopsticks

These are used to place and adjust the small pieces such as eyes, mouths and eyelashes. Tweezers with pointed tips are useful. The chopstick is used to make indentations in rice.

Tsum Tsum Sushi Basics & Tips

INGREDIENTS

These basic tips will make your job a lot easier!
It will be useful if you prepare the ingredients that are to be rolled into equal lengths of roughly 4 inches / 10 cm.

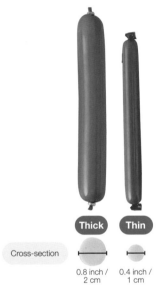

Thick	Thin

Cross-section

0.8 inch / 2 cm	0.4 inch / 1 cm

Fish sausage

The recipes use two types of fish sausage and will indicate which one you should use. Measurements are an estimate. Additionally, depending on where you live, you may not be able to find thin sausages. In that case, you can use thick sausage and cut it to fit your needs. Experimenting is part of the fun.

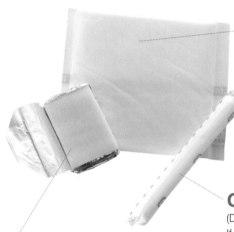

Cheese slices

(Roughly 3 x 3 inches / 8 x 8 cm)
Sliced cheese can vary from country to country. What works best here is any soft, flat cheese that is easily cut. Any individually wrapped white American cheese should work.

Cheese stick

(Diameter roughly 0.4 inch / 1 cm)
If you cannot find perfectly round cheese sticks, you can substitute string cheese—though it is not a perfect circle—or block cheese. See the notes with each individual recipe for how to best substitute.

Processed cheese

(Roughly 1.2 x 1.6 x 0.4 inches / Roughly 3 x 4 x 1 cm)
The foil-wrapped cheese in the photos may be hard to find outside Japan. Any hard white cheese that is at least 4 inches long should work as a substitute.

Kelp cooked in sweet soy sauce

Soy sauce-seasoned kelp, or *kombu*, is difficult to find outside of Japan. You'll want to make your own. It's easy to make at home and you can use it on other dishes as well.

How to make Sweet Soy Sauce Seasoned Kelp

Soak 15 g / 0.5 oz dried Kombu in water, cut into 1 inch squares, simmer in 1/2 cup water + 1/2 tsp rice vinegar, 3 tbsp soy sauce, 1 tbsp sake, 1 tbsp mirin, 1 tbsp sugar.

The thick, dark-colored ones are easier to punch shapes through.

A note on ingredients!

Outside of Japan, different regions are going to have different styles of ingredients available. Some ingredients, such as Deco Furi, may not be easy to find. While you can find a lot of what you need online, some substitution may be necessary. We have provided suggested swaps for ingredients that may not be readily available at your local Japanese market or grocery store. Get creative and make substitutions wherever you see fit!

Red pickled ginger blocks or sushi ginger slices

You can also substitute pink sushi ginger for some recipes, such as Daisy's ribbon.

Pickled burdock root

You will use the section with the right diameter for whatever part you need. Carrots can also be substituted.

Kamaboko fish cake

Choose a plain white one.

Chikuwa

Choose one with a thinner diameter.

Use natural dyes for the food coloring

We recommend you use food dyes made from natural ingredients any time you wish to use food coloring to add color to rice or other ingredients. But natural food dyes tend to be less colorful compared to artificial food coloring, so it is important to adjust the amount of dye you use and the time you dye the ingredient in it.

Natural blue food dye made from gardenia pigments.

It helps to dilute the dye in a small amount of water.

Basic vinegared rice (White)

Making good vinegared rice is the first preparation of making sushi rolls! Pour sushi vinegar (vinegar mixture) over the steamy rice, which has been cooked firmly. Fold the rice and vinegar together and fan it to cool the rice down and remove any excess moisture.

INGREDIENTS for roughly 1.3 lbs. / 600 g

Rice: 360 ml

Water: 360 ml

Sushi vinegar: 60 ml
(Check the chart below for the vinegar mixture recipe)

Sushi vinegar
You can quickly make vinegared rice by pouring this over the hot rice.

PREPARATION

Cook rice at a 1:1 water ratio.

5.3 oz / 150 g of rice = 180 ml (volume)

Usually the amount of water used to cook rice is 10 percent to 20 percent more than the rice, which will result with the rice becoming roughly 2.3 times heavier than before it was cooked. Less water is used to cook sushi rice since the rice needs to be firmer, so the cooked rice will be roughly twice as heavy.

The sushi vinegar / vinegar mixture needed depending on the amount of cooked rice

Rice	Water	Amount of cooked rice	Sushi vinegar	Vinegar mixture		
				Rice vinegar	Sugar	Salt*
5.3 oz / 150 g	180 ml	10.6 oz / 300 g	2 tablespoons (30 ml)	1 1/2 tablespoon	1 tablespoon	1/2 teaspoon
10.6 oz / 300 g	360 ml	1.32 lbs. / 600 g	4 tablespoons (60 ml)	3 tablespoons	2 tablespoons	1 teaspoon
1 lbs. / 450 g	540 ml	2 lbs. / 900 g	6 tablespoons (90 ml)	4 tablespoons	3 tablespoons	1 1/2 teaspoons

*Use less salt when coloring rice with flavored ingredients.

Sushi basic tip!

To create the vinegar mixture, first add the salt into the rice vinegar, stir well, and then add the sugar and stir until it has completely melted. The salt and vinegar will melt quicker if you slightly warm the vinegar.

1

Use the rice paddle to divide the rice into six equal parts.

2

Pour the needed amount of sushi vinegar (vinegar mixture) evenly over the rice.

3

Quickly flip the rice cooker pot over and transfer the rice into a large bowl.

4

Quickly mix the rice from the outside by folding the rice gently from the bottom of the bowl.

5

Fan the rice to cool the rice down.

6

Once the rice has cooled down, place a moist towel over it to avoid drying.

How to make colored vinegared rice

Colorful vinegared rice will add variety to the sushi rolls. The richness of the colors are especially important for the Tsum Tsum sushi rolls in order to add reality to the characters.

A ROUGH GUIDE ON THE AMOUNT YOU NEED TO COLOR THE RICE.

Use these as a reference for the color of the rice that will result when each ingredient is mixed into 1.8 oz / 50 g of vinegared rice (white). Make adjustments as needed to create the color you are aiming for, and add gradually as the color and consistency can change quickly.

Pink

Sweet shellfish flakes (*oboro*), pink fish flakes (*sakura denbu*), pickled plum paste (*neri ume*), salted cod roe (*tarako*), etc.

Sweet shellfish flakes, 1 tablespoon

Pink fish flakes, 1 teaspoon

Orange

Flying fish roe (*tobiko*), salmon flakes*, etc.

*Depending on the type of salmon used, salmon flakes can either be orange or pink.

Flying fish roe, 1 tablespoon

Salmon flakes, 1 tablespoon

Green

Wasabi flavored flying fish roe (*wasabi tobiko*), powdered seaweed (*aonori*), chopped greens, etc.

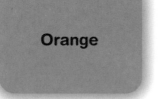
Wasabi flavored flying fish roe, 1 tablespoon

Powdered seaweed, 1 teaspoon

Yellow

Egg threads, pumpkin powder, curry powder, etc.

Egg threads, 1 tablespoon

Brown

Bonito rice seasoning (*katsuo furikake*), dried bonito flakes (*katsuo bushi*), etc.

Bonito rice seasoning, 1 tablespoon

Black

Ground black sesame, purple shiso seasoning (*yukari*)

Ground black sesame, 1 teaspoon

Purple shiso seasoning, 1 teaspoon

Purple

Purple sweet potato powder, purple shiso seasoning (*yukari*), etc.

Red

Powdered shrimp, red pickled plum, etc.

Powders made from dried vegetables such as pumpkin and purple sweet potato.

Light peach

Ground white sesame, etc.

Color the rice easily with Deco Furi or food coloring!

Food coloring and seasonings known as Deco Furi are a shortcut to creating colored vinegared rice. In case Deco Furi is not easy to get ahold of where you are, we recommend food coloring instead. You may need to adjust the amount to best match colors.

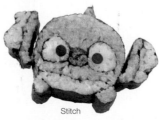

Sulley

Deco Furi provided by Hagoromo Foods

Stitch

About Nori

Nori are an essential part of the sushi roll. Here we will teach you some basic tips how to handle them.

THE SIZE AND FRONT/BACK OF A NORI

You will be using toasted nori sheets for the sushi roll. The common size of a full-size nori sheet is width 7–8 inches / 18–20 cm and length 8–9 inches / 20–22 cm. Make sure to check the front and back of the nori. The front side of the nori should be facing down upon the sushi mat so the front side will be facing outward upon completion.

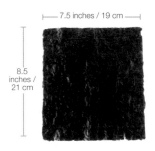

7.5 inches / 19 cm

8.5 inches / 21 cm

The smooth, shiny side is the front and the coarse side is the back.

Front

Back

*The size of the nori sheet may differ depending on the product, but this cookbook will use the above standard.

PREPARATION OF THE NORI / HOW TO CUT IT

Before creating the rolls, cut the nori to size and place them in a can or zipper bag with a desiccant packet to keep them dry.

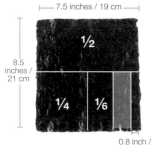

7.5 inches / 19 cm

8.5 inches / 21 cm

½

¼   ⅙

0.8 inch / 2 cm

Example of nori cut for a specific recipe

Cut the full-size nori sheet in half horizontally (1/2). Cut the remaining bottom half (1/2) vertically (1/4). Cut the remaining quarter in half (1/8) and cut the remaining piece into a 0.8 inch / 2 cm strip.

Recommended!
Beginners should definitely use a pair of kitchen scissors. It will help you cut the smaller pieces precisely.

When using a kitchen knife, place the nori sheet on a dry cutting board, place your hand upon the blade and cut the nori with the whole blade.

If you try to cut the nori with the tip by pulling the knife, the nori will get stuck and you will end up with jagged sides.

Full size

Half-size nori that have already been cut in preparation to make sushi rolls.

HOW TO CONNECT THE NORI SHEETS

Connect the nori sheets together if you need a size larger than the 1/2 sheet. If you see "connect the 1/2 and 1/4 nori sheet together" in the recipe, place a few rice grains on the edge of the 1/2 sheet, stretch it out, and then place around 0.4 inch / 1 cm of the 1/4 sheet upon it to connect them together.

HOW TO PLACE THE NORI

The basic rule of making sushi roll is to place the nori upon the sushi mat and then place vinegared rice upon it before you roll it.

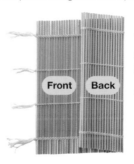

The smooth side (the skin side of the green bamboo) is the front.

*In different regions of Japan, what is considered the front and back of a sushi mat may differ, but this cookbook will use the above rule.

Rolling the sushi roll

When placing the sushi mat down to roll it away from you, make sure the knots are placed at the further end so you do not accidentally wrap the strings into the sushi roll. Also, make sure the edge of the nori sheet is aligned with the bottom of the sushi mat. The same goes for when you are rolling a horizontally long nori sheet and a small nori sheet.

When folding the nori sheet over from both sides

Place the sushi mat sideways with the knots facing the right and place the nori sheet in the middle of the sushi mat.

Basic Preparations

Preparing is very important to smoothly creating Tsum Tsum sushi rolls! Cut the nori sheets into the designated sizes (→ p. 22), divide the vinegared rice into precise portions, and create the small pieces used for the eyes, nose and eyelashes in advance.

WEIGHING THE VINEGARED RICE

The first step is dividing the rice into precise portions. Divide the rice into the designated amounts and arrange the portions in order of size and color so you don't get confused.

It will make the work easier if you are wearing embossed plastic gloves since the rice will not stick to your fingers!

1

Close your fingers and gently scoop the rice so the rice at the bottom does not get squashed.

2

Weigh the rice.

3

Divide the rice into small portions and arrange them in size.

Vinegar water

If you are not going to use plastic gloves, prepare some vinegar diluted water so the vinegared rice will not stick to your hand.

Dip your fingers in the vinegar water and rub it over your palm and between your fingers. Be careful not to rub too much on your hand since it will make the rice mushy.

PREPARING THE SMALL PIECES

You will need to punch and cut out the facial pieces for the eyes and nose, which you will use to decorate the roll later. Even the slightest difference in shape will give the Tsum Tsum a different expression, so it may be a good idea to prepare some spare pieces as extras.

Punch out with a straw

Use a straw to punch circles, ovals and triangles out of ingredients like the soy sauce kelp and fish sausages which are too thick for the nori sheet puncher. As you can see on the right, we use four types of different straws, so be sure to note their sizes. Each straw has been cut into lengths of 1–2 inches / 3–4 cm for convenience.

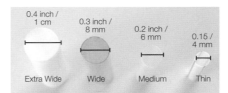

0.4 inch / 1 cm	0.3 inch / 8 mm	0.2 inch / 6 mm	0.15 / 4 mm
Extra Wide	Wide	Medium	Thin

Circle

Push the straw down onto the ingredient from above for circles.

Oval

Slightly squeeze the straw to punch out the ovals.

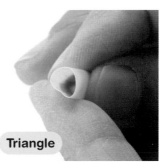

Triangle

Flatten three sides of the straw to punch out the triangles.

Push the pieces out with the tip of a chopstick or bamboo skewer. It is more efficient if you punch out several parts before pushing them all out at once.

(The pieces for the eyebrows and nose)

Punch a circle out and then use the straw to cut an arc shape out of the bottom of the circle.

(Thick eyebrows)

Punch a circle out and cut the top and bottom off with the straw to use the thickest piece in the middle as the thick eyebrow.

Cutting with a bamboo skewer

Use the tip of a bamboo skewer to draw the shape you want to cut out of the soft cheese slice.

Draw the shape with the cheese slice still on its wrapper.

Push the cheese from behind the wrapper to remove the shape.

Attention!

Place the cutout piece in the refrigerator after removing it from the cheese slice. Be careful because it can lose its shape once the cheese softens in room temperature.

Use a bamboo skewer when cutting out thin strands of cheese.

How to roll the sushi roll

How to roll and shape each part of the Tsum Tsum sushi roll.

PLACING AND SPREADING THE RICE ONTO THE NORI

It is easier if you roughly shape the rice before placing it on the nori sheet. Follow each recipe, molding the rice into triangles or stick shapes as directed, and then place on the nori. You may need to spread the rice fully over the nori, halfway over the nori or partly on the nori depending on the recipe.

Stick shape at the bottom of the nori sheet

A triangular mound about 0.8 inch / 2 cm away from the edge of the nori sheet.

Spread the rice evenly over the nori sheet.

Spread the rice on the top half of the nori sheet with more rice in the middle and less rice near the top edge.

A round mound about 2 inches / 5 cm wide in the middle of the nori.

THIN SUSHI ROLLS IN VARIOUS SHAPES

Master the techniques that will help you create various Tsum Tsum sushi rolls!

Round

1 Place the vingared rice at the bottom of the nori sheet in a stick shape and lift up the bottom of the sushi mat which is facing you.

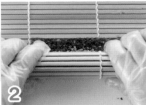

2 Align the bottom of the sushi mat with the farther end of the vinegared rice and roll tightly by pulling your fingers back toward yourself.

3 Slightly lift up the end of the sushi mat and roll the mat forward to complete the sushi roll.

4 Push down upon the vinegared rice on the side to flatten the surface.

Attention!

You can create a nice, round sushi roll by wrapping the completed roll in the sushi mat and rubbing the mat together up and down.

Triangle

Roll it just like the round sushi roll and shape it into a triangle at the end.

Square

Roll it just like the round sushi roll and shape it in a square at the end.

Tear drop

1 Spread the rice on the top half of the nori sheet with more rice in the middle and less rice near the top edge.

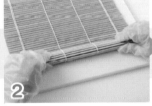

2 Lift up the bottom of the sushi mat facing you and fold it over, pushing gently where the two edges of the nori meet to create a pointed tip.

Oval

1 Place the vinegared rice at the bottom of the nori sheet in an oval stick shape and lift up the bottom of the sushi mat which is facing you.

2 Lift up the bottom of the sushi mat facing you and roll it over.

3 Shape the roll into an oval.

How to make it without the sushi mat

Place a heap of rice along the center of the nori sheet.

Wrap the nori sheet from the top and bottom to create an oval shape.

THICK ROLL

There are a couple of different ways to best roll sushi. You can place the sushi mat flat and then roll away from you. Or you can place the mat sideways and lift the ends of the roll up one at a time. See below for instructions.

Sushi mat placed vertically

Align the nori sheet with the bottom of the sushi mat and place the stick shaped vinegared rice on the bottom of the nori sheet.

Lift the bottom of the sushi mat while holding the vinegared rice and align the bottom of the nori sheet with the far end of the rice.

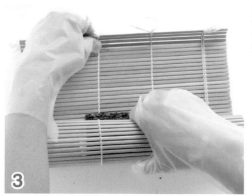

Roll tightly by pulling the sushi roll together with the mat back towards yourself.

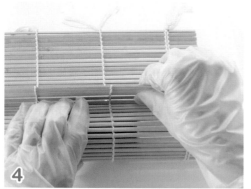

Slightly lift up the end of the sushi mat and roll the mat forward to complete the sushi roll.

Sushi mat placed sideways

Sushi mat placed on surface

Lift up one end of the sushi mat, place that side of the nori sheet onto the roll and press down.

Open the sushi mat again.

Layer the other end of the sushi mat on the roll and wrap the nori around it.

Wrap the sushi mat tightly to shape the roll.

THICK ROLL

Place the sushi mat on your hand and hold it up in a U-shape.

Wrap one side of the nori sheet with the sushi mat.

Flip the other side of the sushi mat over to wrap the nori around tightly.

Attention!

Whichever method you use, you can wrap the sushi roll tightly by flattening a few rice grains along the edge of the nori sheet and using them as glue.

SHAPING THE ROLL AFTER WRAPPING THE SUSHI ROLL

The completed sushi rolls will be in various shapes such as circles and ovals. After the roll is done, place it on the edge of the sushi mat to fix its shape.

Place the sushi roll in the middle of the sushi mat along the edge.

Gently wrap the sushi mat around it and pat down on the side of the roll to flatten it.

For intricate shaped rolls, wrap the sushi mat around the roll to gently shape it.

For the more subtle details, remove the roll from the sushi mat, take a look at the roll from the front and shape the roll with your hand.

29

Cutting

The trick to cutting the sushi roll is to wipe the kitchen knife clean frequently and to move the knife back and forth when cutting it.

HOW TO CUT A SUSHI ROLL

Mark the sushi roll in four places before cutting them in order.

Preparation

Do not forget to prepare a wet cloth and wipe the kitchen knife as often as you can. Slightly moisten the knife first and wipe the rice off every time you cut a slice off the sushi roll. The same goes for cutting a thin sushi roll.

Mark the sushi roll lightly with the tip of the knife before cutting the roll into four equal slices.

First cut the slice off the right end.

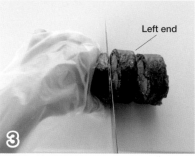

Next, flip the sushi roll over so the left end is facing the right and cut the second slice off the roll.

Finally, cut the remaining roll in half and you will have four equal slices.

Cutting sushi rolls with decorations that are not symmetrical

Cut off about 0.2 inch / 5 mm off the front side of the decoration.

Mark the sushi roll lightly with the tip of the knife before cutting the roll into four equal slices.

Cut into four equal slices from the right side.

All four slices have the same decorative illustrations.

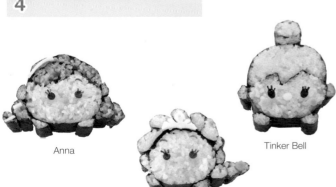

Anna

Elsa

Tinker Bell

HOW TO CUT THE THIN ROLLS AND VARIOUS PARTS

Cut the sushi roll into the number of slices or shapes that you need.

Cutting into equal portions

When cutting two thin sushi rolls into four pieces each, first cut the two rolls in half.

Line up the four sushi rolls and cut those in half to get eight pieces.

Attention!

The nori sheet wrapped around the sushi roll is still crunchy soon after you've rolled it. It will become easier to cut once you leave it for a while and the nori has softened. If you don't want to wait, wrap the sushi roll in a moist towel and moisten the nori before cutting it.

Cutting the sushi roll lengthwise

Create a cut, lengthwise, along the sushi roll with the tip of the knife.

Push the knife down and quickly cut the sushi roll in half.

Finishing Touches

The Tsum Tsum sushi roll is complete when you have placed the hands, ears, and facial features.

CONNECTING THE PARTS

Push down and make sure each part has stuck to the nori sheet.

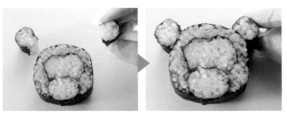

Place the rice side down onto the nori and push down on it for a while.

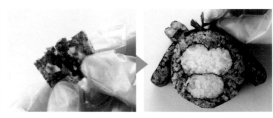

Push down until the nori stick to each other.

Spread out rice grains as glue to connect unique-shaped pieces as well as to connect the whole sushi roll together more firmly.

PLACING THE DECORATIVE PIECES

Where you place the facial features, as well as how well-balanced they are, will determine the subtle difference of the character's expression. Place them carefully!

1 Place the nose in the middle of the face, and then the eyes.

2 Place the eyebrows while paying attention to creating a well-balanced face.

3 Place each strand of eyelash onto the face.

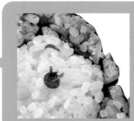

Attention!

Place the eyelashes on the eye and adjust their lengths slightly. If the eyelash seems too long, pull it down onto the eye more to shorten it.

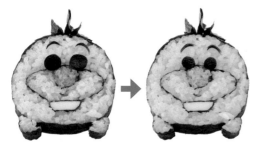

If Olaf's facial expression was not what you imagined after placing the eyes, change the size of the eyes. He looks much cuter with smaller eyes.

Freezable!

The Tsum Tsum sushi rolls can be kept in the freezer if you wrap them up tightly in plastic film. Thaw them at room temperature and eat them as soon as they are thawed.

Tightly wrap them with plastic film. Place them inside a freezer bag, seal the bag airtight and freeze them.

Mickey Mouse

Mickey's famous face, including his round cheeks and big eyes, is iconic. Don't forget to keep his small hands symmetrical.

DIFFICULTY 2
♥ ♥ ♥

actual size

INGREDIENTS FOR FOUR SLICES

Vinegared Rice

Vinegared Rice (White), 0.35 oz / 10 g

Vinegared Rice (Light Beige), 5.3 oz / 150 g
(Vinegared rice 5.1 oz / 145 g + Ground white sesame 0.18 oz / 5 g)

Vinegared Rice (Black) 5 oz / 140 g
(Vinegared rice 4.4 oz / 125 g + Ground black sesame 0.53 oz / 15 g)

Ingredients

Kelp cooked in sweet soy sauce, 2 slices (eyes, nose)

Nori Sheets

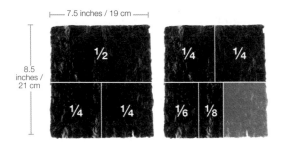

|← 7.5 inches / 19 cm →|

8.5 inches / 21 cm

½ ¼ ¼
¼ ¼ ⅙ ⅛

PREPARATION

Separate the vinegared rice into the various needed portions.

1.8 oz / 50 g × 3   0.35 oz / 10 g

1.4 oz / 40 g × 3   0.7 oz / 20 g

Squeeze the straw slightly to punch out the eyes and nose from the soy sauce kelp.

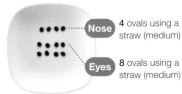

Nose 4 ovals using a straw (medium)

Eyes 8 ovals using a straw (medium)

1. Creating the body parts

Ears

Place vinegared rice (black), 1.4 oz / 40 g, in a stick shape, on the bottom of the 1/4 nori sheet and create two sushi rolls.

Hands

Place vinegared rice (white), 0.35 oz /10 g, in a stick shape on the 1/8 nori sheet, roll and cut it lengthwise in half.

Face

Place vinegared rice (light beige), 1.8 oz / 50 g, in a stick shape on the 1/4 nori sheet and roll into a sushi roll.

2
Cut open the sushi roll lengthwise without cutting through the nori at the bottom.

3
Spread vinegared rice (light beige), 1.5 oz / 50 g, onto the 1/4 nori sheet and curl the side edges up slightly.

4
Place vinegared rice (light beige), 1.5 oz / 50 g, in a stick shape, along the center and cover that with 2.

5
Divide vinegared rice (black), 0.7 oz / 20 g, into three portions. Use them to fill in the dented area on the top and sides and shape the face into an oval.

2. Assemble and Roll

1
Stretch a few rice grains out along the edge of the 1/2 nori sheet and overlap around 0.4 inch / 1 cm of the 1/6 sheet upon it to connect the nori together.

2
Spread vinegared rice (black), 1.4 oz / 40 g, evenly onto the nori but leave about 2.4 inches / 6 cm open on both sides. Place the face onto it with the nori surface facing up.

3
Keeping the sushi mat laid out, lift up one side (starting from the left side) and wrap the nori around the face.

4
Lift up the other side (right side) and wrap it around the roll.

3. Cutting and Finishing Touches

1
Align the sushi roll with the edge of the sushi mat, gently wrap to adjust the shape of the roll and pat the side to flatten it.

2
Mark the sushi roll lightly with the tip of the knife before cutting the roll into four equal slices.

3
First slice off the right end, flip the sushi roll over so the left end is facing the right and continue to cut the other slices.

4
Cut both rolls for the ears and hands into four pieces each.

5
Push the ears and hands firmly onto the face and connect them.

6
Place the eyes and nose on the face.

Attention! Place the eyes and nose slightly below the center of the face.

CHANGE THE EXPRESSION!!
★★★★★★★★★★★★★★★
Winking Mickey. The soy sauce kelp has been cut into a > shape for one eye.

Mickey (Back)

Mickey's little tail always sticks out of his cute red pants. It points to the left.

DIFFICULTY 1

Vinegared Rice

Vinegared Rice (Red) 6.7 oz / 190 g
(Vinegared rice 6.2 oz / 175 g + Deco Furi (red) 0.53 oz / 15 g)

Vinegared Rice (Black), 3.8 oz / 110 g
(Vinegared rice 3.5 oz / 100 g + black ground sesame 0.35 oz / 10 g)

Ingredients

Kelp cooked in sweet soy sauce, 1 slice (tail)

Nori Sheets

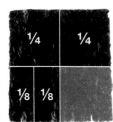

7.5 inches / 19 cm

8.5 inches / 21 cm

½ ¼ ¼

½ ⅛ ⅛

PREPARATION

Separate the vinegared rice into the various needed portions.

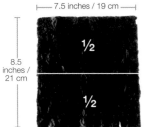

7.05 oz / 190 g

1.4 oz / 40 g x 2

0.7 oz / 20 g

0.35 oz / 10 g

Cut the soy sauce kelp into tail shapes.

Tail — Roughly 0.6 inch / 1.5 cm, **4** strands

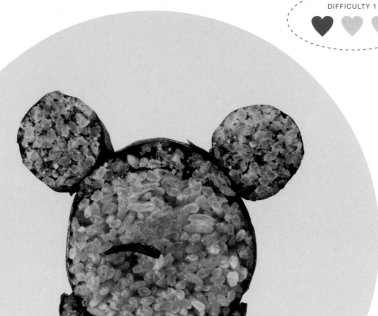

actual size

1. Creating the body parts

Ears

Place vinegared rice (black) 1.4 oz / 40 g, in a stick shape, on the bottom of the 1/4 nori sheet and create two sushi rolls.

Feet

Place vinegared rice (black), 0.35 oz / 10 g, in a stick shape on the 1/8 nori sheet, roll and cut it lengthwise in half.

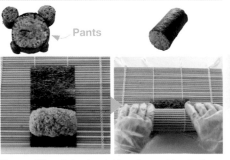

Pants

Place a 1/2 nori sheet upright on the sushi mat, place vinegared rice (red), 7.05 oz / 190 g, on the nori in a stick shape and wrap into a sushi roll.

2. Assemble and Roll

1 Place the sushi mat sideways on the table. Connect the 1/2 and 1/8 nori sheet together, place it on the sushi mat, and put the pants roll in the middle of the nori.

2 Cover the top with vinegared rice (black) 0.7 oz / 20 g and shape it onto a dome-shape.

3 Keeping the sushi mat laid out, lift up one side (starting from the left side) and wrap the nori around the face.

4 Lift up the other side (right side) and wrap it around the roll.

3. Cutting and Finishing Touches

1 Align the sushi roll with the edge of the sushi mat, gently wrap to adjust the shape of the roll and pat the side to flatten it.

2 Cut the sushi into four even slices, wiping the knife with a cloth after each cut.

3 Cut the each of the ears and feet sushi roll into four pieces and attach them to the pants roll.

4 Place the tail in the center and point it to the left.

FRONT
****
1 slice of Mickey's face (→ p. 34) and two slices of Mickey's back!

BACK
****

Minnie Mouse

Minnie's face is the same shape as Mickey's, but she also has eyelashes and pink cheeks. Don't forget the polka dots on her big red ribbon.

DIFFICULTY 2 ♥ ♥ ♡

actual size

INGREDIENTS FOR FOUR SLICES

Vinegared Rice

Vinegared Rice (White), 0.35 oz / 10 g

Vinegared Rice (Light Beige), 5.3 oz / 150 g
(Vinegared rice 5.1 oz / 145 g + ground white sesame 0.18 oz / 5 g)

Vinegared Rice (Black), 5 oz / 140 g
(Vinegared rice 4.4 oz / 125 g + ground black sesame 0.53 oz / 15 g)

Vinegared Rice (Red), 1.06 oz / 30 g
(Vinegared rice 1.06 oz / 30 g + a dash of Deco Furi (red))

Ingredients

Fish sausage (thin* / 4 inches or 10 cm), 1 sausage (center of the ribbon, cheeks)

*If you do not have thin fish sausage, you can use thick sausages and cut them to fit.

Cheese slice, 1/4 slice (ribbon's polka dots)

Kelp cooked in sweet soy sauce, 2 slices (eyes, nose)

Nori Sheets

← 7.5 inches / 19 cm →

8.5 inches / 21 cm

| ½ |
| ¼ | ¼ |

| ¼ | ¼ |
| ⅛ | ⅛ | ⅛ | ⅛ |

| ⅙ |

PREPARATION

Separate the vinegared rice into the various needed portions.

1.8 oz / 50 g x 3   0.35 oz / 10 g

0.53 oz / 15 g x 2

1.4 oz / 40 g x 3   0.7 oz / 20 g

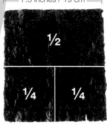

Eyelashes

24 strands. Cut extremely thin eyelashes out from the remaining nori sheet snippets.

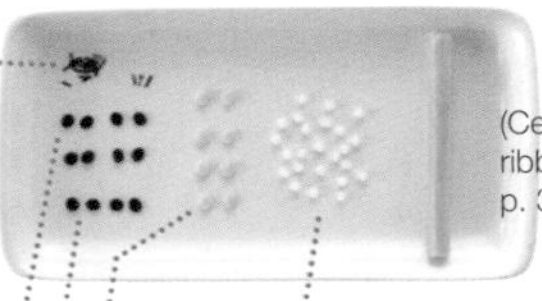

(Center of the ribbon → p. 39/ribbon)

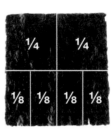

Polka dots   24 dots using a straw (thin)

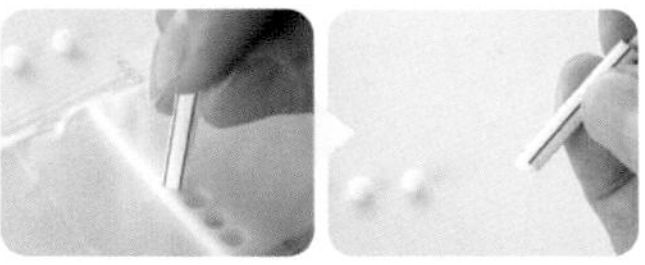

Use a straw to punch the eyes and nose out of the soy sauce kelp. Punch the cheeks out of the fish sausage and the dots out of the cheese slice.

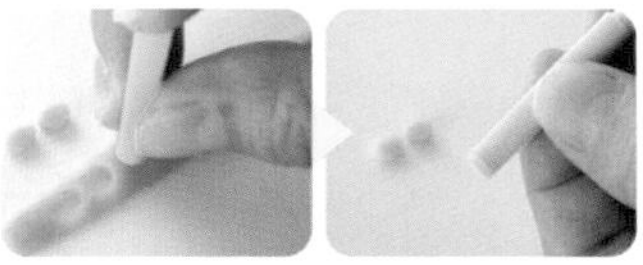

Eyes   8 ovals using straw (medium)

Nose   4 ovals using straw (medium)

Cheeks   8 ovals using straw (medium)

*Punched out of the remains of the sausage after removing the center of the ribbon.

1. Creating the body parts

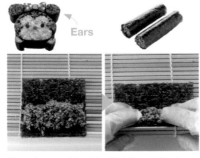

→ Ears

Place vinegared rice (black), 1.4 oz / 40 g, in a stick shape, on the bottom of the 1/4 nori sheet and create two sushi rolls.

← Hands

Place vinegared rice (white), 0.35 oz / 10 g, in a stick shape on the 1/8 nori sheet, roll and cut it lengthwise in half.

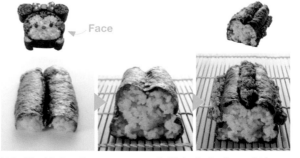

→ Face

Make Minnie's face the same way you do Mickey's. (→ See p. 34.)

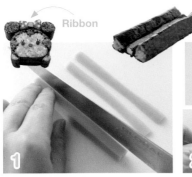

Ribbon

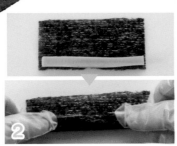

1 Cut the sides of the fish sausage, so the cross-section would be a square.

If using a thicker sausage or hot dog, use the sample photo above as reference and cut to match the size and shape as closely as possible.

2 Wrap it with the 1/8 nori sheet.

3 Place vinegared rice (red), 0.53 oz / 15 g, in a stick shape on the 1/8 nori sheet and create two triangular rolls.

4 Attach 3 on both sides of 2 to create a ribbon shape.

2. Assemble and Roll (p. 35 Same as Mickey)

1 Connect the 1/2 and 1/6 nori sheet, spread vinegared rice (black), 1.4 oz, onto the nori, leaving 2.4 inches / 6 cm on both sides, and place the face in the middle.

2 Keep the sushi mat on the table and wrap the nori around the roll by flipping each side of the sushi mat over.

3. Cutting and Finishing Touches

1 Align the sushi roll with the edge of the sushi mat, gently wrap to adjust the shape of the roll and pat the side to flatten it.

2 Cut the sushi into four even slices, wiping the knife with a cloth after each cut.

3 Cut both rolls for the ears and hands into four pieces and attach two of each onto the face.

4 Cut the ribbon into four even pieces, place it in between the ears and add the polka dots to it.

5 Place the eyes, nose and cheek on the face.

6 Place three strands of eyelashes on each eye.

CHANGE THE EXPRESSION!!
★★★★★★★★★★★★★★★★★
Cute winking Minnie.

MICKEY & MINNIE

Minnie (Back)

Minnie's white bloomers peek out of her skirt.

actual size

DIFFICULTY 2
♥ ♥ ♥

INGREDIENTS FOR FOUR SLICES

Vinegared Rice

Vinegared Rice (White), 3.9 oz / 110 g

Vinegared Rice (Red), 4.6 oz / 130 g
(Vinegared rice 4.2 oz / 120 g + Deco Furi (red) 0.35 oz / 10 g)

Vinegared Rice (Black), 3.2 oz / 90 g
(Vinegared rice 3 oz / 85 g + ground black sesame 0.18 oz / 5 g)

Ingredients

Fish sausage (thin / 4 inches or 10 cm), 1 sausage
(center of the ribbon)

Cheese slice, 1/4 slice (ribbon's polka dots)

Kelp cooked in sweet soy sauce, 1 slice (tail)

Nori Sheets

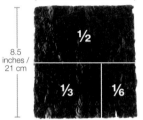 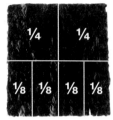

← 7.5 inches / 19 cm →

8.5 inches / 21 cm

1/2

1/3 1/6

1/4 1/4

1/8 1/8 1/8 1/8

PREPARATION

Separate the vinegared rice into the various needed portions.

1.4 oz / 40 g x 2   0.35 oz / 10 g

3.5 oz / 100 g   0.53 oz / 15 g x 2   3.9 oz / 110 g

(Center of the ribbon →
p. 39/ribbon)

Tail

Roughly 0.6 inch / 1.5 cm, **4** pieces
Cut the soy sauce kelp into tail shapes.

Polka dots

24 dots using a straw (thin)
Use a straw to punch out the polka dots from the cheese slice.

1. Creating the body parts

Ears

Place vinegared rice (black) 1.4 oz / 40 g, in a stick shape, on the bottom of the 1/4 nori sheet. (Create two of these.)

Feet

Place vinegared rice (black) 0.35 oz / 10 g, in a stick shape on the 1/8 nori sheet, roll and cut it lengthwise in half.

Ribbon

Same as Minnie's ribbon (→ p. 39).

2. Assemble and Roll

1 Place a 1/2 nori sheet upright on the sushi mat, place vinegared rice (white) 3.9 oz / 110 g, on the nori in a stick shape.

2 Wrap into a round sushi roll.

3 Connect the 1/2 and 1/6 nori sheet, spread vinegared rice (red) 3.5 oz / 100 g on the nori leaving 0.4 inch / 1 cm on the left and 2.4 inches / 6 cm on the right.

4 Use a chopstick to create six vertical dents in the rice.

5 Place 2 in the middle, flip over each side of the nori and wrap the sushi roll.

6 Remove from the sushi mat and use a chopstick to add clearer dents to the roll.

3. Cutting and Finishing Touches

1 Align the sushi roll with the edge of the sushi mat, gently wrap to adjust the shape of the roll and pat the side to flatten it.

2 Cut the sushi into four even slices, wiping the knife with a cloth after each cut.

3 Adjust the shape the roll to add the frills of the skirt.

4 Cut the ears and feet rolls into four pieces and attach them.

5 Cut the ribbon into four even pieces, place it in between the ears, and add the polka dots to it.

6 Place the tail in the center and point it slightly to the low left.

Donald Duck

Place Donald's signature hat on his head with a slight slant. He will look even cuter if his yellow beak, eyes, and cheek are positioned a little closer to the bottom of his face!

DIFFICULTY 2

actual size

Vinegared Rice

Vinegared Rice (White), 6.7 oz / 190 g

Vinegared Rice (Red), 0.7 oz / 20 g
(Vinegared rice 0.7 oz / 20 g + a dash of Deco Furi (red))

Vinegared Rice (Yellow), 0.7 oz / 20 g
(Vinegared rice 0.7 oz / 20 g + a dash of pumpkin powder)

Vinegared Rice (Blue), 0.53 oz / 15 g
(Vinegared rice 0.53 oz / 15 g + a dash of Deco Furi (sky))

Ingredients

Kelp cooked in sweet soy sauce, 1 slice (eyes)

Sliced ham, 1/4 slice (roughly)
You could also use fish sausage here for the cheeks.

Nori Sheets

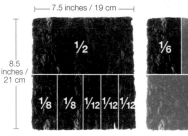

PREPARATION

Separate the vinegared rice into the various needed portions.

1.8 oz / 50 g x 2   0.35 oz / 10 g

2.82 oz / 80 g   0.29 oz / 8 g x 2

0.53 oz / 15 g   0.7 oz / 20 g   0.14 oz / 4 g

Eyes

8 ovals using a straw (wide)
Squeeze the straw slightly to punch out the eyes and nose from the soy sauce kelp and the cheeks from the sliced ham.

Cheeks

8 ovals using a straw (medium)

Ribbon for Hat

4 sets. Cut out the ribbons for the hat from the remaining nori snippets.

1. Creating the body parts

Hands

Place vinegared rice (white) 0.35 oz / 10 g, in a stick shape on the 1/8 nori sheet, roll and cut it lengthwise in half.

Beak

Place vinegared rice (yellow) 0.7 oz / 20 g on the 1/6 size nori, spread it out in a width of 1.2 inches / 3 cm, wrap the nori from both sides to create an oval-shaped sushi roll.

Hat

Create a 4 inch / 10 cm long stick out of the vinegared rice (blue) 0.53 oz / 15 g and place a 1/8 nori sheet over it.

Ribbon

1 Create a 4 inch / 10 cm long triangular stick out of vinegared rice (red) 0.28 oz / 8 g.

2 Fold a 1/12 nori sheet in half and cover the triangular stick. (Create two of these.)

3 Place vinegared rice (red), 0.14 oz / 4 g, on a 1/12 nori sheet and create a sushi roll.

4 Place the triangles from **2** to the sides of **3** to create a ribbon.

2. Assemble and Roll

1 Place the sushi mat sideways on the table. Place a 1/2 nori sheet on it and spread the vinegared rice (white), 1.8 oz / 50 g, out in the middle of the nori in a width of 2.4 inches / 6 cm.

2 2.82 oz / 80 g — Place the beak in the middle. Spread the 2.82 oz / 80 g vinegared rice out with the palm of your hand and cover the beak with it.

3 1.8 oz / 50 g — Add another 1.8 oz / 50 g of vinegared rice on top of that and form it into a dome shape.

4 Keep the sushi mat on the table and wrap the nori around the roll by flipping each side of the sushi mat over.

3. Cutting and Finishing Touches

1 Align the sushi roll with the edge of the sushi mat, gently wrap to adjust the roll into an oval shape and pat the side to flatten it.

2 Cut the sushi roll into four even slices while wiping the kitchen knife with a wet cloth.

3 Cut the hat into four pieces and connect slightly off center to the right.

4 Apply the ribbon to the hat.

5 Cut each roll of the ribbon and hands into four pieces and attach them.

6 Place the eyes and cheeks on the face.

CHANGE THE EXPRESSION!!
★★★★★★★★★★★★★★★
Change his eyes into a cute pink heart. Cut the hearts out of ham slices.

Attention! Donald will look cuter if you place the eyes and cheeks close to his beak.

Daisy Duck

Daisy has similar features to Donald but don't forget her longer eyelashes and larger eyes. Her pink ribbon is cute, too.

DIFFICULTY 2
♥ ♥ ♥

actual size

INGREDIENTS FOR FOUR SLICES

Vinegared Rice

Vinegared Rice (White), 7.05 oz / 200 g

Vinegared Rice (Yellow), 0.7 oz / 20 g
(Vinegared rice 0.7 oz / 20 g + a dash of pumpkin powder)

Ingredients

Red Pickled Ginger (Thick Slice) as needed (ribbon)
You could also substitute a think piece of pink gari, or possibly ham or fish sausage, here for a similar effect.

Kelp cooked in sweet soy sauce, 1 slice (eyes)

Sliced ham, 1/4 slice (cheeks)

Nori Sheets

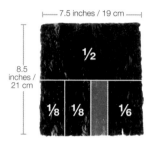

├── 7.5 inches / 19 cm ──┤

8.5 inches / 21 cm

½

⅛ ⅛ ⅙

PREPARATION

Separate the vinegared rice into the various needed portions.

2.82 oz / 80 g

1.8 oz / 50 g x 2

0.35 oz / 10 g x 2

0.7 oz / 20 g

Eyelashes
24 strands. Cut extremely thin eyelashes out from the remaining nori sheet snippets.

Eyes
8 ovals using a straw (wide).
Squeeze the straw slightly to punch out the eyes and the cheeks from the ham.

Cheeks
8 ovals using straw (medium)

Ribbon
4 sets. Cut the red pickled ginger into ribbon shapes.

1. Creating the body parts

Hands

Place vinegared rice (white), 0.35 oz / 10 g, in a stick shape on the 1/8 nori sheet, roll and cut it lengthwise in half.

Beak

Place vinegared rice (yellow), 0.7 oz / 20 g, on the 1/6 size nori, spread it out in a width of 1.2 inches / 3 cm, wrap the nori from both sides to create an oval shaped sushi roll.

Base of the Ribbon

Wrap vinegared rice (white), 0.35 oz / 10 g, with a 1/8 nori sheet, into a round sushi roll. Cut almost in half, leaving the other side of the nori intact then spreading the cut roll open.

2. Assemble and Roll

1 Place the sushi mat sideways on the table. Place a 1/2 nori sheet on it and spread the vinegared rice (white), 1.8 oz / 50 g, out in the middle of the nori in a width of 2.4 inches / 6 cm.

2 Place the beak in the middle. Spread the 2.82 oz / 80 g vinegared rice out with the palm of your hand and cover the beak with it.

2.82 oz / 80 g

3 Add another 1.8 oz / 50 g of vinegared rice on top of that and shape it into a dome-shape.

1.8 oz / 50 g

4 Keep the sushi mat on the table and wrap the nori around the roll by flipping each side of the sushi mat over.

3. Cutting and Finishing Touches

1 Align the sushi roll with the edge of the sushi mat, gently wrap to adjust the roll into an oval shape and pat the side to flatten it.

2 Cut the sushi roll into four even slices, wiping the kitchen knife with a wet cloth after each cut.

3 Place the base for the ribbon on the top of the head and attach the ribbon to it.

4 Cut the hand sushi rolls into four even pieces each and attach two of them to each face.

5 Place the eyes on the face and attach 3 strands of eyelashes to the eyes.

6 Place the cheeks on the face.

Attention! Prepare the eyelashes in long strands and adjust their lengths by how much you overlap them onto the eyes.

CHANGE THE EXPRESSION!!
★★★★★★★★★★★★★★★
Place eyelashes onto the winking eye to add even more cuteness!

DONALD & DAISY

Pluto

A yellow face, round eyes and long drooping black ears are Pluto's most recognizable characteristics. Make the eyes look like an elongated heart and connect it to the nose.

actual size

INGREDIENTS FOR FOUR SLICES

Vinegared Rice

Vinegared Rice (White), 2.1 oz / 60 g

Vinegared Rice (Yellow), 5.3 oz / 150 g
(Vinegared Rice 5.1 oz / 145 g + Deco Furi (yellow), 2 packs)

Vinegared Rice (Black), 1.4 oz / 40 g
(Vinegared rice 1.23 oz / 35 g + ground black sesame 0.18 oz / 5 g + a dash of purple shiso seasoning)

Ingredients

Kelp cooked in sweet soy sauce, 2 slices (eyes, nose)

Nori Sheets

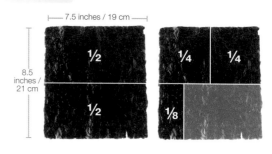

PREPARATION

Separate the vinegared rice into the various needed portions.

Use a straw to punch the eyes and nose out of the soy sauce kelp.

Nose 4 ovals using a straw (wide)

Eyes 8 circles using a straw (medium)

1. Creating the body parts

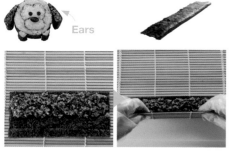
Ears

Place a 1/2 nori sheet sideways, spread the vinegared rice (black) 1.4 oz / 40 g in a width of 1.6 inches / 4 cm and fold the nori over itself.

Hands

Place vinegared rice (yellow) 0.35 oz / 10 g, in a stick shape on the 1/8 nori sheet, roll and cut it lengthwise in half.

Nose

Place vinegared rice (yellow) 1.4 oz / 40 g on the 1/4 size nori sheet and wrap into an oval sushi roll.

Eyes & Nose

1 Place vinegared rice (white) 1.8 oz / 50 g, in a stick shape, on the 1/4 nori sheet and wrap it into a sushi roll.

2 Cut open the sushi roll lengthwise without cutting through the nori at the bottom.

3 Place vinegared rice (yellow), 0.18 oz / 5 g, on the dent at the top, and add vinegared rice (white), 0.35 oz / 10 g, to the rice inside the roll at the bottom.

4 Place 3 on top of the nose and examine the overall shape, adjusting as needed.

2. Assemble and Roll

1 Spread vinegared rice (yellow), 2.1 oz / 60 g, on top of the 1/2 size nori sheet leaving 1.2 inches / 3 cm open on both ends and place the eyes and nose in the middle.

0.35 oz / 10 g

2 Use the remaining 0.35 oz / 10 g portions of vinegared rice (yellow) to create a stick shape and fill in the dents on both sides.

0.53 oz / 15 g

3 Flatten the vinegared rice (yellow) 0.53 oz / 15 g, cover the top of the roll with it and shape the rice around the roll into a dome.

4 Keep the sushi mat on the table and wrap the nori around the roll by flipping each side of the sushi mat over.

3. Cutting and Finishing Touches

1 Place the just rolled side at the bottom, shape the sushi roll into an oval and flatten the sides.

2 Cut the sushi roll into four even slices, wiping the kitchen knife with a wet cloth after each cut.

3 Cut the ears into 8 pieces and each of the hands into 4 pieces.

4 Attach the long ears as if they are drooping down.

5 Attach the left and right hands.

6 Place the nose and eyes on the face.

Attention! Placing the larger facial features located in the center of the face first will make it easier for you to create a well-balanced face.

CHANGE THE EXPRESSION!!
Try a mischievous-looking Pluto with his tongue poking out.

Goofy

Goofy's key features are his long ears, the slightly slanted hat and the three strands of hair poking out at the top. Just like Pluto, his eyes should look like a heart-mark when creating his face.

actual size

INGREDIENTS FOR FOUR SLICES

Vinegared Rice

Vinegared Rice (White), 2.46 oz / 70 g

Vinegared Rice (Black), 4.6 oz / 130 g
(Vinegared rice 4.2 oz / 120 g + ground black sesame 0.35 oz / 10 g + a dash of purple shiso seasoning)

Vinegared Rice (Beige), 1.4 oz / 40 g
(Vinegared rice 1.4 oz / 40 g + dash of Deco Furi (yellow and orange))

Vinegared Rice (Green), 0.53 oz / 15 g
(Vinegared rice 0.53 oz + a dash of Deco Furi (green))

Ingredients

Kelp cooked in sweet soy sauce, 2 slices (eyes, nose)

Nori Sheets

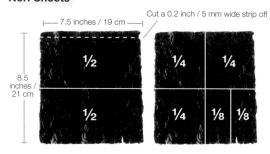

Cut a 0.2 inch / 5 mm wide strip off

7.5 inches / 19 cm

8.5 inches / 21 cm

½ ½ ¼ ¼ ¼ ⅛ ⅛

PREPARATION

Separate the vinegared rice into the various needed portions.

Use a straw to punch the eyes and nose out of the soy sauce kelp.

Nose 4 ovals using a straw (extra wide)

Eyes 8 circles using a straw (medium)

2.1 oz / 60 g   1.06 oz / 30 g   0.53 oz / 15 g

1.4 oz / 40 g

0.35 oz / 10 g x 2   0.18 oz / 5 g

1.8 oz / 50 g   0.53 oz / 15 g

0.35 oz / 10 g x 2

1. Creating the body parts

 **Hat**

Wrap 2/3 of the vinegared rice (green) (0.35 oz / 10 g) with a 1/8 size nori sheet and wrap into a sushi roll. Cut the sushi roll open lengthwise, keeping the opposite side of the nori intact.

Use the remaining vinegared rice to create a thin stick shape and place that in the roll.

Flip the roll over push the dent down and shape into a hat.

 Three strands of hair

Spread several grains of rice over a 1/4 size nori sheet while leaving 0.4 inch / 1 cm on the top and bottom open.

Fold the center of the nori sheet into a mountain fold that is 0.4 inch / 1 cm tall.

Fold the remaining sides into 0.4 inch / 1 cm tall mountain folds too to create three strands of hair.

 **Hands**

Place vinegared rice (white) 0.35oz / 10 g, in a stick shape on the 1/8 nori sheet, roll and cut it lengthwise in half.

 **Nose**

Place vinegared rice (beige) 1.4 oz / 40 g on the 1/4 nori sheet and wrap into an oval.

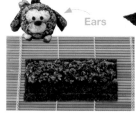 **Ears**

Place a 1/2 nori sheet (with a 0.2 inch / 5 mm wide strip cut off it) sideways, spread the vinegared rice (black) 1.06 oz / 30 g in a width of 1.6 inches / 4 cm and fold the nori over itself.

1 Place vinegared rice (white) 1.8 oz / 50 g, in a stick shape, on the 1/4 nori sheet and wrap it into a sushi roll.

2 Cut open the sushi roll lengthwise, keeping the opposite side of the nori intact.

3 Place vinegared rice (black) 0.18 oz / 5 g on the dent at the top, and add vinegared rice (white) 0.35 oz / 10 g to the rice inside the roll at the bottom.

4 Place **3** on top of tho nose and examine the overall shape, adjusting as needed.

2. Assemble and Roll

1 Spread vinegared rice (black) 2.1 oz / 60 g on top of the ½ size nori sheet leaving 1.2 inches / 3 cm open on both ends.

2 Place the eyes and ears in the middle and fill in the dents on the side by stretching the two 0.35 oz / 10 g vinegared rice (black) portions into a stick shape.

3 Flatten the vinegared rice (black) 0.53 oz / 15 g, cover the top of the roll with it and shape the rice around the roll into a dome.

4 Keep the sushi mat on the table and wrap the nori around the roll by flipping each side of the sushi mat over.

3. Cutting and Finishing Touches

1 With the bottom of the roll facing down, shape the sushi roll into an oval and flatten the side.

2 Cut the sushi roll into four even slices, wiping the kitchen knife with a wet cloth after each cut.

3 Cut the ears into 8 pieces and each of the hands and hair into 4 pieces.

4 Cut the hat into four pieces and cut the 0.2 inch / 5 mm wide strip into 1.2 inch / 3 cm long pieces, then wrap the strips around the bottom of each hat.

5 Attach the ears to the sides and place the hat on tho left side.

6 Glue the three strands of hair firmly onto the roll using flattened rice as glue.

7 Attach the hands and place the nose and eyes on the face.

CHANGE THE EXPRESSION!!

Look! Goofy is so surprised that his hat has flown off!

49

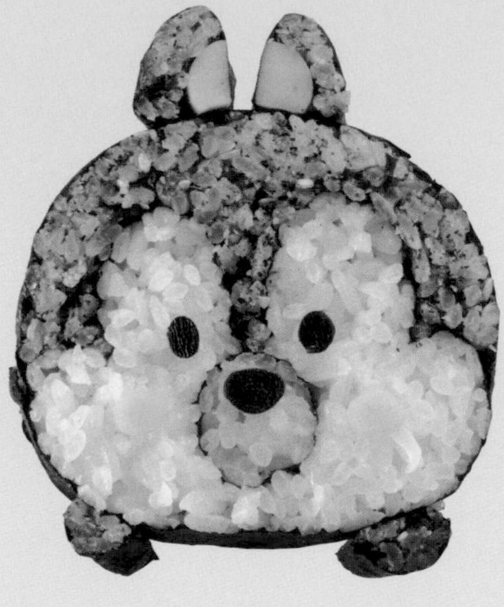

Chip

actual size

The insides of Chip's cute pointy ears are pink. Take care when rolling the area around his nose, eyes and cheeks!

DIFFICULTY 2

INGREDIENTS FOR FOUR SLICES

Vinegared Rice

Vinegared Rice (White), 4.76 oz / 135 g

Vinegared Rice (Dark Brown), 3.56 oz / 101 g
(Vinegared rice 3.2 oz / 90 g + ground black sesame 0.18 oz / 5 g + bonito rice seasoning 0.21 oz / 6 g)

Ingredients

Fish sausage (thin / 4 inches or 10 cm), 1 sausage (ears, cheek)

Kelp cooked in sweet soy sauce, 2 slices (eyes, nose)

Nori Sheets

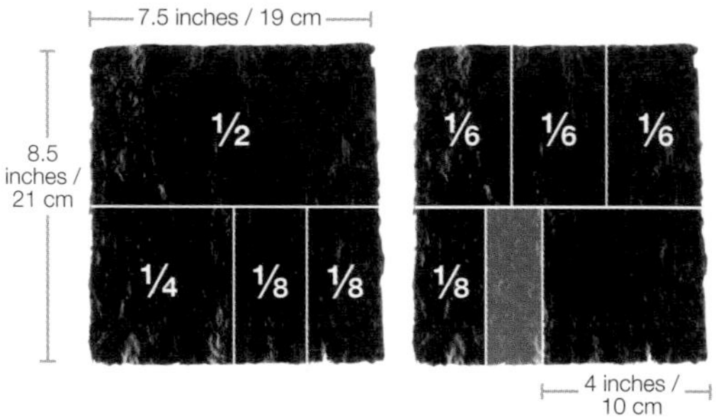

7.5 inches / 19 cm
8.5 inches / 21 cm
½
¼
⅛
⅛
⅙
⅙
⅙
⅛
4 inches / 10 cm

PREPARATION

Separate the vinegared rice into the various needed portions.

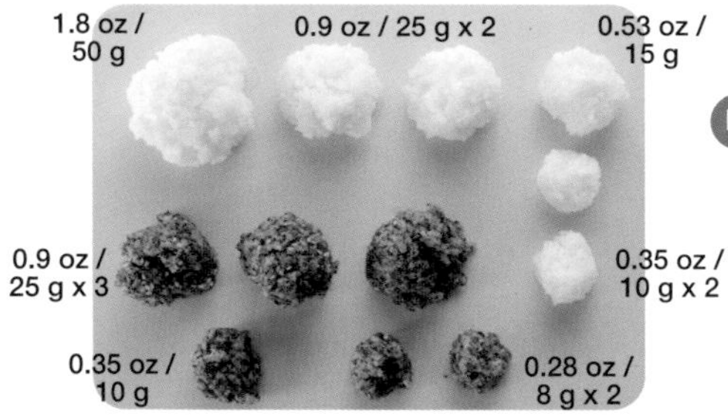

1.8 oz / 50 g
0.9 oz / 25 g x 2
0.53 oz / 15 g
0.9 oz / 25 g x 3
0.35 oz / 10 g x 2
0.35 oz / 10 g
0.28 oz / 8 g x 2

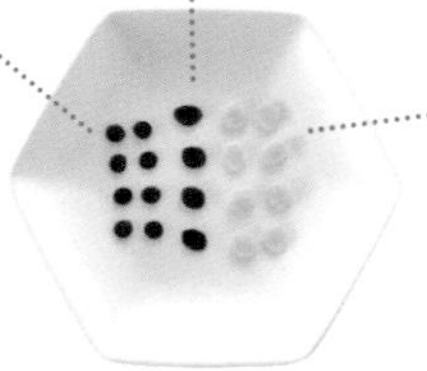

Eyes 8 ovals using a straw (medium)

Nose 4 ovals using a straw (wide)

Cheeks 8 ovals using a straw (wide) Use the scraps leftover from the ears.

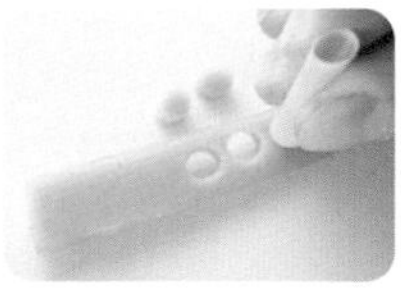

Squeeze the straw slightly to punch the eyes out of the soy sauce kelp and the cheeks out of the fish sausage.

1. Creating the body parts

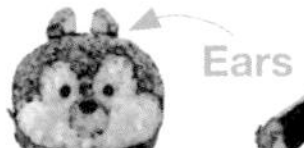

Ears

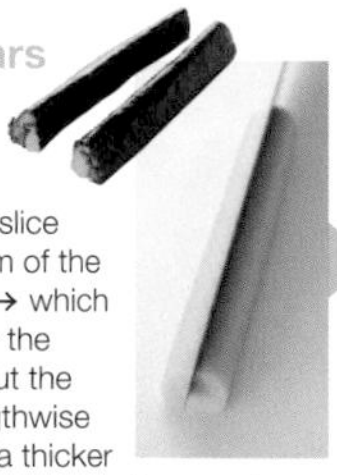

Remove a thin slice from the bottom of the fish sausage (⟶ which will be used for the cheeks), and cut the upper part lengthwise in half. If using a thicker sausage or hotdog, use the sample photo above as reference and cut to match the size and shape as closely as possible.

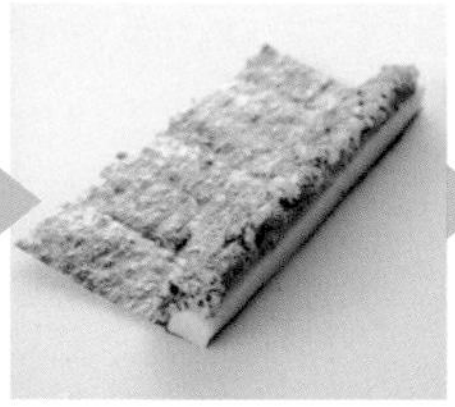

Place the sausage on the edge of a 1/8 size nori and cover it with vinegared rice (dark brown) 0.28 oz / 8 g.

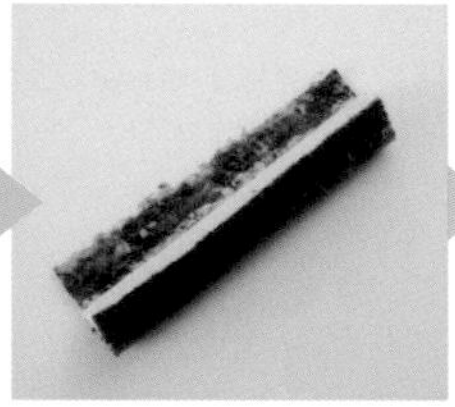

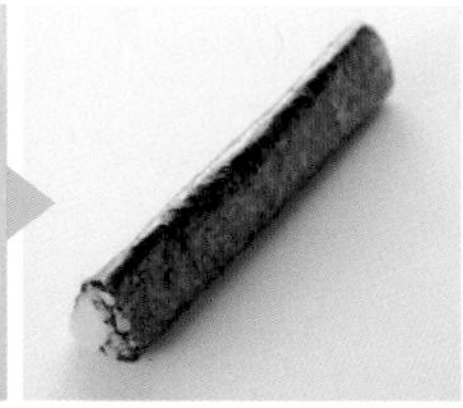

Wrap the nori around it and close the roll. (Create two of these.)

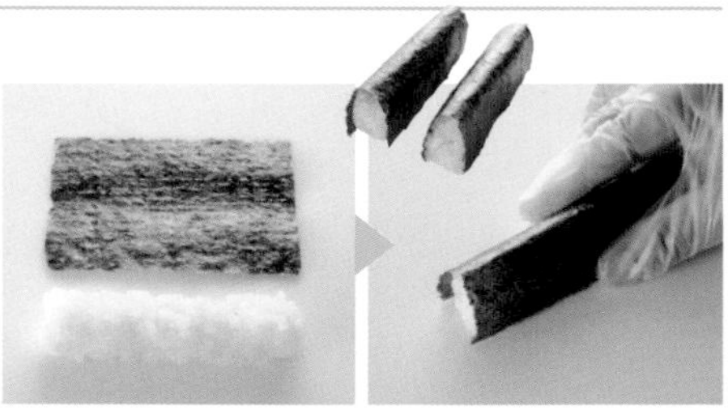

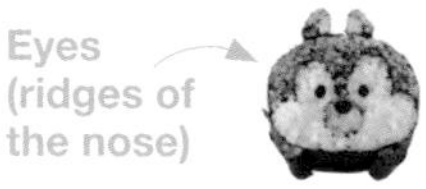

Eyes (ridges of the nose)

Create a 4 inch / 10 cm long stick out of the vinegared rice (white) 0.9 oz / 25 g and place a 1/6 size nori sheet over it. (Create two of these.)

Attention!

Both ears are wrapped in the same way, but it will save you some time if you place them side by side with the pink sausage both facing the inside in preparation for the cutting and attaching.

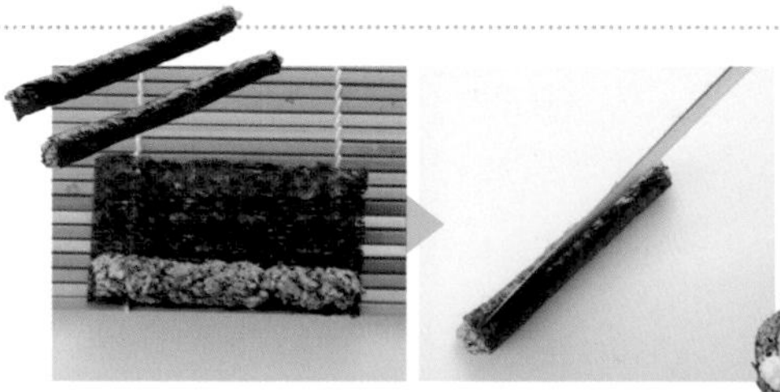

Place the vinegared rice (dark brown) 0.35 oz / 10 g, in a stick shape on the 1/8 nori sheet, roll and cut it lengthwise in half.

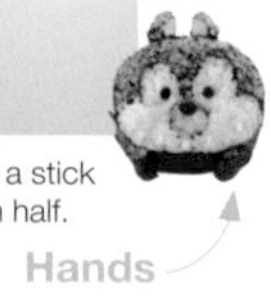

Hands

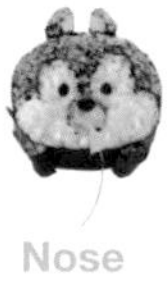

Nose

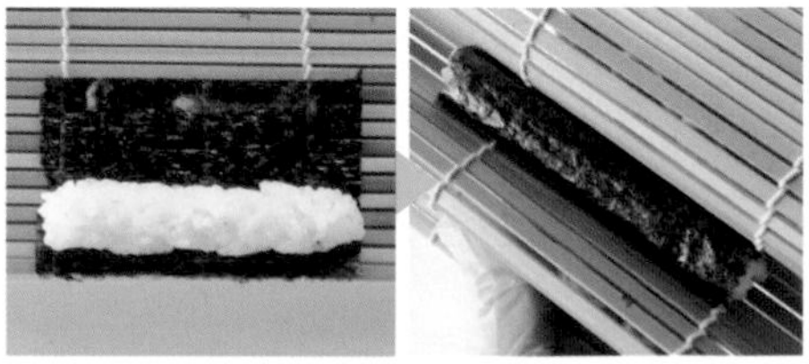

Place vinegared rice (white) 0.53 oz / 15 g, in a stick shape on the 1/6 nori sheet and wrap into a sushi roll.

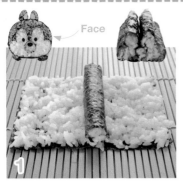

Face

1 Spread vinegared rice (white) 1.8 oz / 50 g evenly over the 4 inch / 10 cm wide nori sheet and place the nose in the middle.

2 Sandwich 1 from both sides with vinegared rice (white) 0.35 oz / 10 g on either side.

3 Place the eyes (ridges of the nose) on top of 2 and wrap the cheeks from both sides.

4 Use the sushi mat to press against each side and form the shape of the face.

2. Assemble and Roll

1 Connect the 1/2 and 1/4 size nori sheet, put it on the sushi mat which has been placed sideways. Place the face in the center of the nori.

0.9 oz / 25 g   0.9 oz / 25 g   0.9 oz / 25 g

2 Place vinegared rice (dark brown) 0.9 oz / 25 g in the space between the eyes and another 0.9 oz / 25 g to the sides of each eye.

3 Connect the rice together into a dome shape.

4 Keep the sushi mat on the table and wrap the nori around the roll by flipping each side of the sushi mat over.

3. Cutting and Finishing Touches

1 Align the sushi roll with the edge of the sushi mat, gently wrap to adjust the roll into an oval shape and pat the sides to flatten.

2 Cut the sushi roll into four even slices, wiping the kitchen knife with a wet cloth after each cut.

3 Adjust the shape of the face into a slightly wide oval while fixing the curves around the cheeks and any misshapes along the ridges of the nose.

4 Cut each of the ears and hands into four equal pieces.

5 Attach the ears while paying attention to which way they are facing, and also place the hands on the face.

6 Place the nose, eyes, and cheek on the face in that order.

CHANGE THE EXPRESSION!!
★★★★★★★★★★★★★★★★
Try a cute winking Chip with his tongue poking out.

51

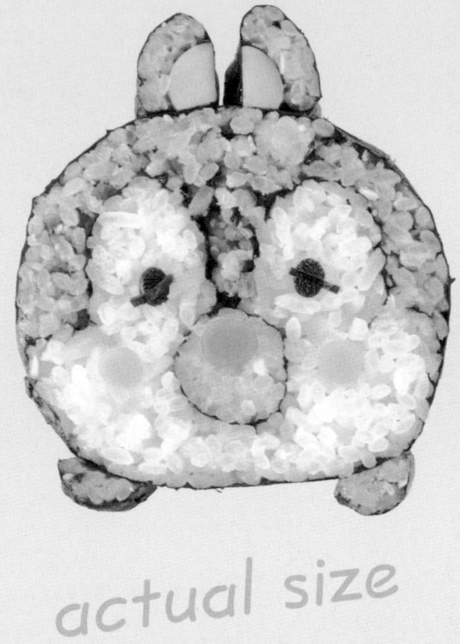
actual size

Dale

Use the same method for Dale as for Chip, but Dale's base color is light brown and his nose is red. A line goes diagonally across the eyes to make him look even more like Dale.

DIFFICULTY 2

INGREDIENTS FOR FOUR SLICES

Vinegared Rice

Vinegared Rice (White), 4.76 oz / 135 g

Vinegared Rice (Light Brown), 3.56 oz / 101 g
(Vinegared rice 3 oz / 85 g + bonito rice seasoning 0.35 oz / 10 g + ground white sesame 0.21 oz / 6 g)

Ingredients

Fish sausage (thin / 4 inches or 10cm), 1 sausage (ears, cheek)

Kelp cooked in sweet soy sauce, 2 slices (eyes, line across the eyes)

Pickled burdock root, 0.8–1.2 inches / 2–3 cm

Nori Sheets

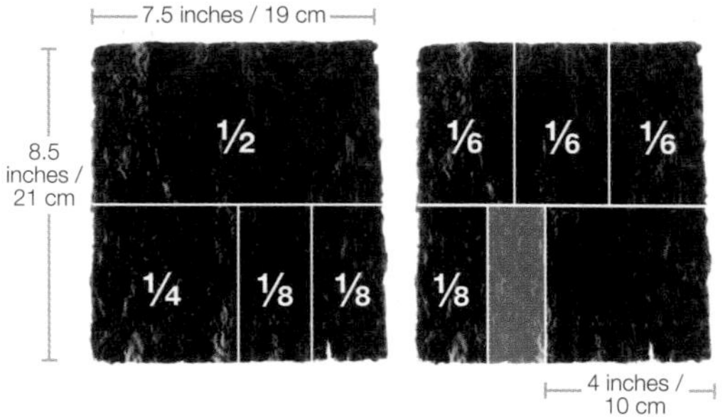
7.5 inches / 19 cm
8.5 inches / 21 cm
½
¼
⅛
⅛
⅙
⅙
⅙
⅛
4 inches / 10 cm

PREPARATION

Separate the vinegared rice into the various needed portions.

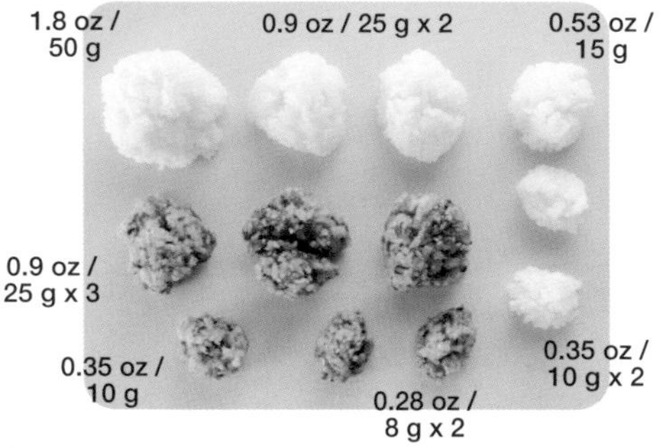
1.8 oz / 50 g
0.9 oz / 25 g x 2
0.53 oz / 15 g
0.9 oz / 25 g x 3
0.35 oz / 10 g
0.28 oz / 8 g x 2
0.35 oz / 10 g x 2

Squeeze the straw slightly to punch the eyes out of the soy sauce kelp and the cheeks out of the fish sausage.

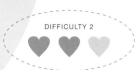

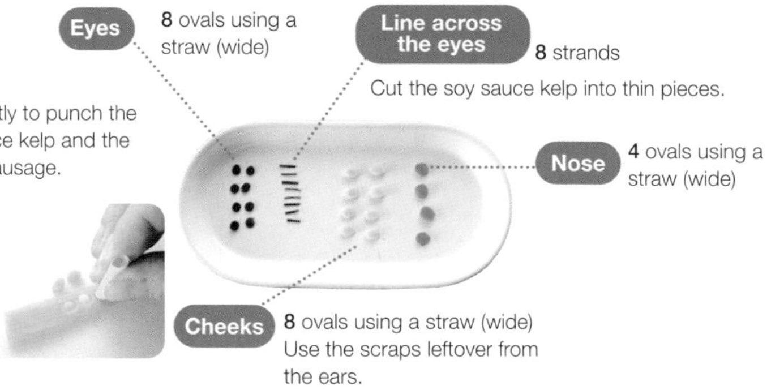
Eyes
8 ovals using a straw (wide)
Line across the eyes
8 strands
Cut the soy sauce kelp into thin pieces.
Nose
4 ovals using a straw (wide)
Cheeks
8 ovals using a straw (wide)
Use the scraps leftover from the ears.

1. Creating the body parts

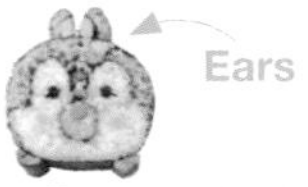
Ears

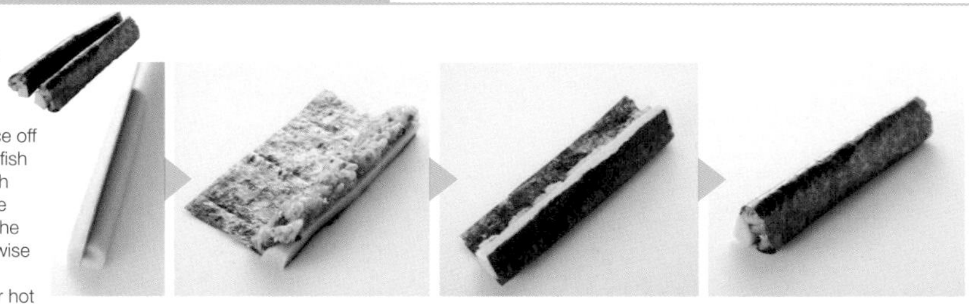

Remove a thin slice off the bottom of the fish sausage (→ which will be used for the cheeks), and cut the upper part lengthwise in half. If using a thicker sausage or hot dog, use the sample photo above as reference and cut to match the size and shape as closely as possible.

Place the sausage on the edge of a 1/8 size nori and cover it with vinegared rice (light brown) 0.28 oz / 8 g.

Wrap the nori around it and close the roll. (Create two of these.)

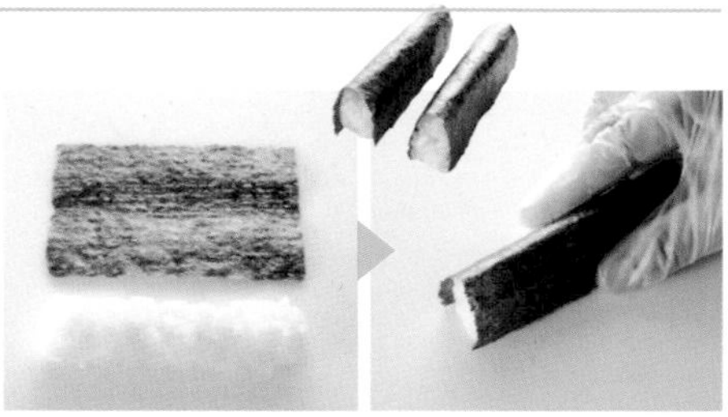

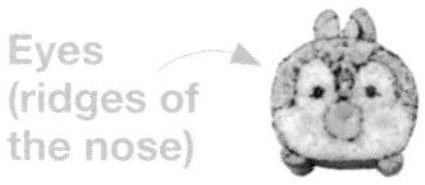
Eyes (ridges of the nose)

Create a 4 inch / 10 cm long stick out of the vinegared rice (white) 0.9 oz / 25 g and place a 1/6 size nori sheet over it. (Create two of these.)

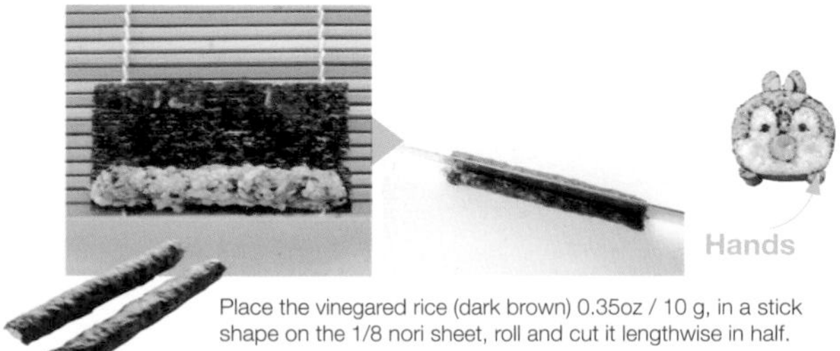
Hands

Place the vinegared rice (dark brown) 0.35oz / 10 g, in a stick shape on the 1/8 nori sheet, roll and cut it lengthwise in half.

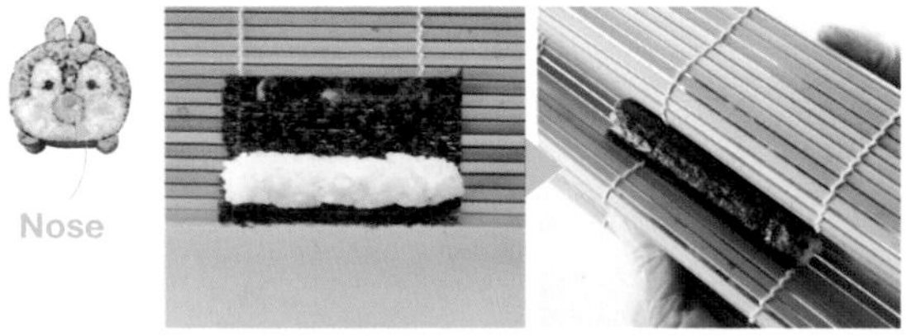
Nose

Place vinegared rice (white) 0.53 oz / 15 g, in a stick shape on the 1/6 nori sheet and wrap into a sushi roll.

Face

1 Spread vinegared rice (white), 1.8 oz / 50 g, evenly over the 4 inches / 10 cm wide nori sheet and place the nose in the middle.

2 Sandwich 1 from both sides with the portions of vinegared rice (white) 0.35 oz / 10 g on either side.

3 Place the eyes (ridges of the nose) on top of 2 and wrap the cheeks from both sides.

4 Use the sushi mat to press against each side and form the shape of the face.

2. Assemble and Roll

1 Connect the 1/2 and 1/4 size nori sheet, put it on the sushi mat which has been placed sideways. Place the face in the center of the nori.

0.9 oz / 25 g   0.9 oz / 25 g   0.9 oz / 25 g

2 Place vinegared rice (light brown), 0.9 oz / 25 g, on the dents on the top of the eyes and the side. in the space between the eyes and another 0.9 oz / 25 g to the sides of each eye.

3 Connect the rice together into a dome shape.

4 Keep the sushi mat on the table and wrap the nori around the roll by flipping each side of the sushi mat over.

3. Cutting and Finishing Touches

1 Adjust the shape of the roll using the sushi mat and cut the roll into four even slices.

2 Cut each of the ears and hands into four pieces.

3 Place the nose, eyes, and the lines across the eyes on the face in that order.

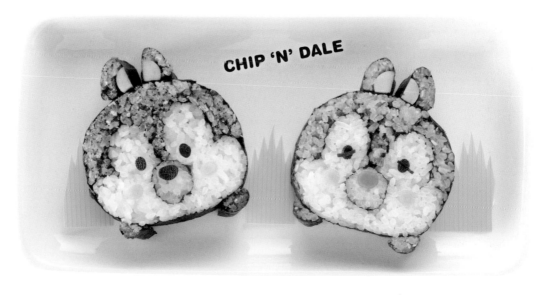

4 Place the cheeks on the face.

CHANGE THE EXPRESSION!!
★★★★★★★★★★★★★★★★
Dale's wink is so cute!!

CHIP 'N' DALE

53

Winnie the Pooh

Create your own Pooh with just a simple round sushi roll using yellow vinegared rice. Pay attention to where you place the eyebrows, eyes and nose.

actual size

Vinegared Rice

Vinegared Rice (Yellow), 8.8 oz / 250 g
(Vinegared rice 8.47 oz / 240 g + Deco Furi (yellow) 0.35 oz / 10 g)

Ingredients

Kelp cooked in sweet soy sauce, 3 slices
(eyebrows, eyes, nose, ridges of the nose)

Nori Sheets

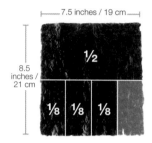

⊢ 7.5 inches / 19 cm ⊣

8.5 inches / 21 cm

½

⅛ ⅛ ⅛

PREPARATION

Separate the vinegared rice into the various needed portions.

7.05 oz / 200 g 0.7 oz / 20 g x 2 0.35 oz / 10 g

Use a straw to punch the eyes, nose and ridges of the nose out.
Cut the eyebrows out of the soy sauce kelp.

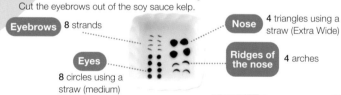

Eyebrows 8 strands

Nose 4 triangles using a straw (Extra Wide)

Eyes 8 circles using a straw (medium)

Ridges of the nose 4 arches

Punch out a circle with a straw (extra wide) and use the straw again to cut off the arc at the bottom of the circle.

1. Creating the body parts

 Ears

 Hands

Place vinegared rice (yellow), 0.7 oz / 20 g, in a stick shape, on the 1/8 nori sheet and wrap it into a sushi roll. (Create two of these.)

Do not wrap the sushi roll all the way and keep it slightly open with the rice still visible.

Place vinegared rice (yellow) 0.35 oz / 10 g, in a stick shape on the 1/8 nori sheet, roll and cut it lengthwise in half.

2. Roll

1. Place a 1/2 size nori sheet upright on the sushi mat and place vinegared rice (yellow) 7.05 oz / 200 g on the bottom end of the nori.

2. Lift the bottom of the sushi mat while holding the vinegared rice.

3. Roll the rice and nori over to the far end and wrap the sushi roll.

3. Cutting and Finishing Touches

1. Align the sushi roll with the edge of the sushi mat, gently wrap to adjust the shape of the roll and pat the sides to flatten.

2. Cut the roll into four equal slices and adjust their shape into a slightly wide oval.

3. Cut the rolls for the ears and hands into four pieces and attach two of each onto the face.

4. Place the nose and ridge of the nose in the contor of the face

5. Place the eyes and eyebrows on.

CHANGE THE EXPRESSION!!
★★★★★★★★★★★★★★★★
Change the eyes to a curved line to make Pooh sleep, zzz.

Piglet

DIFFICULTY 1
♥ ♥ ♥

Piglet has distinctive pointy ears. You just need to create a round roll for his hands and face, so it's very easy!

actual size

INGREDIENTS FOR FOUR SLICES

Vinegared Rice

Vinegared Rice (Light Pink), 7.76 oz / 220 g
(Vinegared rice 7.76 oz / 220 g + a dash of Deco Furi (red))

Ingredients

Kelp cooked in sweet soy sauce, 2 slices
(eyebrows, eyes)

Red pickled ginger (thin slice / 0.39 x 0.39 or 1cm x 1 cm),
4 slices (nose)

Nori Sheets

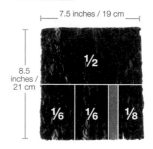

7.5 inches / 19 cm

8.5 inches / 21 cm

½

⅙ ⅙ ⅛

PREPARATION

Separate the vinegared rice into the various needed portions.

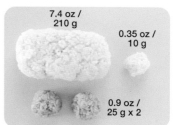

7.4 oz / 210 g

0.35 oz / 10 g

0.9 oz / 25 g x 2

Eyes 8 circles using a straw (medium)

Use a straw to punch the eyes and eyebrows out of the soy sauce kelp.

Eyebrows 8 strands

You can easily punch a circle out using a straw (wide), cut it in half, and then punch the arc out of that.

Nose 4

Cut the red pickled ginger in a triangle and round off the edges.

1. Creating the body parts

Ears

Flat

Rounded

Create a mound that is 4 inches / 10 cm long and 0.8 inch / 2 cm high with the vinegared rice (dark pink) 0.9 oz / 25 g.

Cover it with a 1/6 size nori sheet and adjust its shape so one side is flat and the other side has been rounded. (Create two of these.)

Hands

Place vinegared rice (light pink) 0.35 oz / 10 g, in a stick shape on the 1/8 nori sheet and roll into a sushi roll.

Cut it lengthwise in half.

2. Roll

1 Place a 1/2 size nori sheet upright on the sushi mat and place vinegared rice (light pink) 7.4 oz / 210 g on the bottom end of the nori.

2 Lift the bottom of the sushi mat while holding the vinegared rice. Roll the rice and nori over to the far end and wrap the sushi roll.

3. Cutting and Finishing Touches

1 Align the sushi roll with the edge of the sushi mat, gently wrap to adjust the shape of the roll and pat the sides to flatten.

2 Cut the sushi roll into four even slices, wiping the kitchen knife with a wet cloth after each slice, then adjust the shape of the roll.

3 Cut each of the hands and ears into four pieces.

4 Place the ears on the face with the flat side facing in and also attach the hands.

5 Place the nose and eyes on the face.

Adjust its length after checking how it looks on the face.

6 Place the eyebrows on.

LOTS OF TSUM TSUM SUSHI ROLLS

Can you find Piglet?

CHANGE THE EXPRESSION!!

Try pointing his eyebrows down for a slightly troubled expression.

Tigger

DIFFICULTY 2 ♥ ♥ ♥

Tigger has yellow and orange coloring, thick brows and slightly squared ears. He also has stripes on the outside of his nose that are facing up as well as three whiskers on both sides.

actual size

INGREDIENTS FOR FOUR SLICES

Vinegared Rice

Vinegared Rice (Yellow), 4.94 oz / 140 g
(Vinegared rice 4.76 oz / 135 g + Deco Furi (yellow), 2 packs)

Vinegared Rice (Orange), 3.9 oz / 110 g
(Vinegared rice 3.7 oz / 105 g + Deco Furi (orange), 2 packs)

Ingredients

Kelp cooked in sweet soy sauce, 3 slices
(eyebrows, eyes, stripes)

Pickled burdock root, 0.8–1.2 inches / 2–3 cm (nose)

Nori Sheets

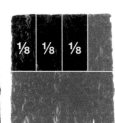

⟵ 7.5 inches / 19 cm ⟶

8.5 inches / 21 cm

½ | ⅛ ⅛ ⅛
¼ ¼

PREPARATION

Separate the vinegared rice into the various needed portions.

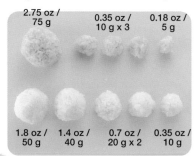

2.75 oz / 75 g | 0.35 oz / 10 g x 3 | 0.18 oz / 5 g

1.8 oz / 50 g | 1.4 oz / 40 g | 0.7 oz / 20 g x 2 | 0.35 oz / 10 g

Use a straw to punch the eyes out of the soy sauce kelp. Then also cut the thick eyebrows and stripes from the kelp.

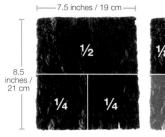

Stripes 8 strands

Eyebrows 8 strands

Eyes 8 ovals using a straw (medium)

Nose 4 triangles using a straw (wide)

Whiskers 24 strands

Cut out extremely thin whiskers from the remaining snippets of nori.

Punch the triangle out from the thinly sliced pickled burdock root.

You can also cut the triangle out with the tip of a knife.

Attention! Leave the roll open so that you can still see the rice inside.

1. Creating the body parts

Ears

Place vinegared rice (yellow), 0.7 oz / 20 g, in a stick shape, on the 1/8 nori sheet and wrap it into a sushi roll.

Hands

Place vinegared rice (orange), 0.35 oz / 10 g, in a stick shape on the 1/8 nori sheet, roll and cut it lengthwise in half.

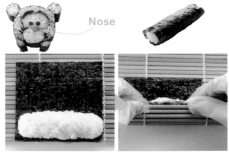
Nose

Place vinegared rice (yellow), 1.4 oz / 40 g on the 1/4 size nori sheet and wrap into an oval sushi roll.

Eyes and Nose

1 Place vinegared rice (yellow), 1.8 oz / 50 g, in a stick shape, on the 1/4 nori sheet and wrap it into a sushi roll.

2 Cut open the sushi roll lengthwise, but do not cut through the nori at the bottom.

3 Place vinegared rice (orange) 0.18 oz / 5 g on the dent at the top, and add vinegared rice (yellow) 0.35 oz / 10 g to the rice inside the roll at the bottom.

4 Place the nose on the bottom of 3 (the side with the yellow vinegared rice) and adjust its shape as needed.

2. Roll

1 Spread vinegared rice (orange) 2.75 oz / 75 g on top of the 1/2 size nori sheet leaving 1.2 inches / 3 cm open on both ends and place the eyes and nose in the middle.

2 On each side of the face, add 0.35 oz / 10 g of vinegared rice (orange) in a stick shape to fill in the dents.

3 Keep the sushi mat on the table and wrap the nori around the roll by flipping each side of the sushi mat over.

4 Layer the ends of the nori to complete the roll.

3. Cutting and Finishing Touches

1 With the bottom of the face on the mat, shape the sushi roll into an oval and flatten the sides.

2 Cut the sushi roll into four even slices, wiping the kitchen knife with a wet cloth after each cut.

3 Cut the ears into eight pieces and each of the hands into four pieces.

4 Attach two ears and hands onto the face.

5 Place the nose and eyes in that order.

6 Place the eyebrows upon the contours of the eyes.

7 Place one stripe and three strands of whiskers on each side of the contour of the nose.

CHANGE THE EXPRESSION!!

Is he happy? Or is he troubled? What a mischievous face.

59

Eyeore

DIFFICULTY 3
♥ ♥ ♥

Eeyore's mane is made from simmered shiitake mushroom. Use the left over pieces to decorate his face.

actual size

Cut the shiitake mushroom after you've sliced the sushi roll so you can cut it into the right size to balance it out with the face.

INGREDIENTS FOR FOUR SLICES

Vinegared Rice

Vinegared Rice (Purple), 6.35 oz / 180 g
(Vinegared rice 6.35 oz / 180 g + a dash of purple sweet potato powder)

Vinegared Rice (Beige), 2.46 oz / 70 g
(Vinegared rice 2.46 oz / 70 g + a dash of ground white sesame)

Ingredients

Fish sausage (thick / 4 inches or 10 cm), 1 (ears)

Simmered shiitake mushroom (diameter: 1.2 inches / 3 cm), 4 (mane, eyebrows, nose, stitches)

Kelp cooked in sweet soy sauce, 1 slice (eyes)

Nori Sheets

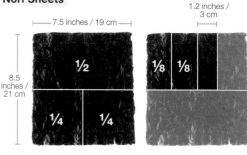

1.2 inches / 3 cm

7.5 inches / 19 cm

8.5 inches / 21 cm

½   ⅛ ⅛

¼   ¼

PREPARATION

Separate the vinegared rice into the various needed portions.

3.5 oz / 100 g   1.8 oz / 50 g   0.35 oz / 10 g x 3

2.46 oz / 70 g

Eyes 8 ovals using a straw (medium)

1. Creating the body parts

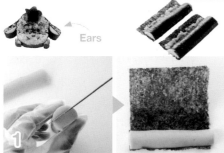

Ears

① Slice 0.2 inch / 5 mm off the top and bottom of the fish sausage lengthwise and place it on the edge of a 1/4 size nori sheet.

② Wrap it once (flat side facing up) and spread vinegared rice (purple) 0.35 oz / 10 g on the nori at a width of 1.4 inches / 3.5 cm and wrap it once again. (Create two of these.)

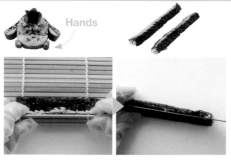

Hands

Place vinegared rice (purple) 0.35 oz / 10 g, in a stick shape on the 1/8 nori sheet, roll and cut it lengthwise in half.

60

2. Assemble and Roll

1 Place vinegared rice (beige) 2.46 oz / 70 g in the middle of a 1/2 nori sheet at a width of 1.6 inches / 4 cm and place a 1/8 size nori sheet on top of it.

2 Shape the vinegared rice (purple) 3.5 oz / 100 g in a width of 1.6 inches / 4 cm and a length of 4 inches / 10 cm.

3 Cut the rice in half and sandwich a 1.2 inches / 3 cm wide strip of nori in between the rice.

4 Make sure the bottom of the nori strip is touching the cutting board and combine the rice back into its original shape.

5 Place 4 on top of 1.

6 Spread the vinegared rice (purple) 1.8 oz / 50 g out and pile it on top of 5.

7 Adjust the shape of the rice into a dome shape.

8 Keep the sushi mat on the table and wrap the nori around the roll by flipping each side of the sushi mat over.

3. Cutting and Finishing Touches

1 Align the sushi roll with the edge of the sushi mat, gently wrap to adjust the shape of the roll and pat the sides to flatten.

2 Cut the sushi roll into four even slices, wiping the kitchen knife with a wet cloth after each cut.

3 Cut each of the hands and ears rolls into four even pieces.

4 Cut the simmered shiitake mushroom onto Eeyore's mane while paying attention to how it looks on the face.

5 Use the scraps left from 4 to cut the pieces for the eyebrows, nose and stitch marks.

6 Attach the ears and hands.

7 Place the eyes, eyebrows, nose and stitches in that order.

CHANGE THE EXPRESSION!!
His eyebrows and eyes make him look sad.

Cooking Shiitake Mushrooms

There are a few different ways to cook shitake mushroom. It could simply be simmered with no seasoning, but typically is cooked with a combination of soy sauce, sake, mirin and dashi. You could also add sugar if you prefer a sweeter mushroom.

Stitch

DIFFICULTY 3
♥ ♥ ♥

Stitch's uniquely shaped ears, with indentations at the top of the right ear and bottom of the left ear, have been re-created in this roll. His large eyes are created from tunnel-shaped rolls!

actual size

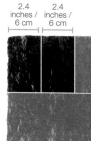

CHANGE THE EXPRESSION!!

Pointy teeth!
Talkative Stitch.

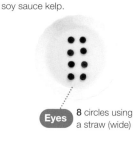

Use a straw to punch the eyes out of the soy sauce kelp.

Eyes 8 circles using a straw (wide)

INGREDIENTS FOR FOUR SLICES

Vinegared Rice

Vinegared Rice (Blue), 6.53oz / 185 g
(Vinegared rice 6 oz / 170 g + Deco Furi (sky) 0.53 oz / 15 g)

Vinegared Rice (Light Blue), 2.82 oz / 80 g
(Vinegared rice 2.82 oz / 80 g + a dash of Deco Furi (sky))

Vinegared Rice (Pink), 1.4 oz / 40 g
(Vinegared rice 1.4 oz / 40 g + a dash of Deco Furi (pink))

Vinegared Rice (Black), 0.35 oz / 10 g
(Vinegared rice 0.35 oz / 10 g + a dash of ground black sesame)

Ingredients

Kelp cooked in sweet soy sauce, 1 slice (eyes)

Nori Sheets

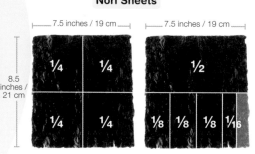

PREPARATION

Separate the vinegared rice into the various needed portions.

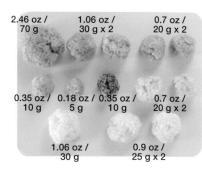

2.46 oz / 70 g   1.06 oz / 30 g x 2   0.7 oz / 20 g x 2

0.35 oz / 10 g   0.18 oz / 5 g   0.35 oz / 10 g   0.7 oz / 20 g x 2

1.06 oz / 30 g   0.9 oz / 25 g x 2

1. Creating the body parts

Eyes

Nose

Hair

Hands

Place vinegared rice (light blue) 0.9 oz / 25 g on a 1/4 size nori sheet and wrap into a tunnel-shaped roll. (Create two of these.)

Place vinegared rice (black) 0.35 oz / 10 g on the 1/8 size nori sheet and wrap into an oval sushi roll.

Shape the vinegared rice (blue) 0.18 oz / 5 g into a 4 inch / 10 cm stick shape and cover it with a 1/16 nori sheet.

Place vinegared rice (blue) 0.35 oz / 10 g, in a stick shape on the 1/8 nori sheet, wrap it into a roll and cut it lengthwise in half.

Attention! The nori sheet is intentionally long. Wrap it around the rice a few times to emphasize the black outer contour of the eyes.

62

Ears

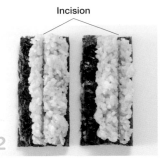  

1 Spread vinegared rice (blue) 0.7 oz / 20 g on one-half of the 1/4 size nori sheet. Fold the nori sheet over to sandwich the rice. (Create two of these.)

Incision

2 Spread vinegared rice (pink), 0.7 oz / 20 g, in a width of roughly 1.2 inches / 3 cm starting from the edge where the nori sheet has been folded over and make a slight incision in the rice at the 2/3 location (left) and 1/3 location (right).

3 Stretch a few grains or rice along both edges of the 2.4 inches / 6 cm nori sheet and cover 2 with it.

4 Create a dent and shape the ear. Create the left ear in the same way too.

2. Assemble and Roll

1 Place the sushi mat sideways and place a 1/2 nori sheet on it. Spread vinegared rice (light blue), 1.06 oz / 30 g, out in a width of 1.6 inches / 4 cm in the center of the nori and cover it with a 1/8 size nori sheet.

2 Spread vinegared rice (blue), 1.06 oz / 30 g, in a width of 1.6 inches / 4 cm.

3 Place the nose in the middle and the eyes on its side and fill in the gap between them using vinegared rice (blue), 1.06 oz / 30 g.

Nose

Eyes

4 Cover it with more vinegared rice (blue) 2.46 oz / 70 g.

5 Shape the rice into a dome shape.

6 Keep the sushi mat on the table and wrap the nori around the roll by flipping each side of the sushi mat over.

3. Cutting and Finishing Touches

1 Align the sushi roll with the edge of the sushi mat, gently wrap to adjust the shape of the roll and pat the sides to flatten.

2 Cut the sushi roll into four even slices, wiping the kitchen knife with a wet cloth after each slice. Adjust the shape of the roll as needed.

3 Cut each roll of the hands, ears and hair into four equal pieces.

4 Attach the ears while paying attention to which side the ear should go on.

5 Attach the hair on the very top of the face and the hands on both sides.

6 Place the eyes near the nose.

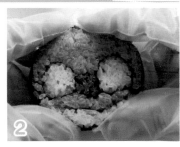

Marie

actual size

Marie is a cute kitty with a large pink ribbon. The fur on both sides of her cheeks is expressed by folding the nori to create creases.

DIFFICULTY 3
♥ ♥ ♥

INGREDIENTS FOR FOUR SLICES

Vinegared Rice

Vinegared Rice (White), 8.47 oz / 240 g

Vinegared Rice (Pink), 10.6 oz / 30 g
(Vinegared rice 1.06 oz / 30 g + a dash of Deco Furi (red))

Ingredients

Fish sausage (thick / 4 inches or 10 cm), 2 sausages (ears, cheek, nose)

Fish sausage (thin / 4 inches or 10 cm), 1 sausage (center of the ribbon)

Kelp cooked in sweet soy sauce, 2 slices (eyes, whiskers)

Nori Sheets

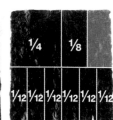

├— 7.5 inches / 19 cm —┤

8.5 inches / 21 cm

½ ¼ ⅛ ¼ ¼ 1/12 1/12 1/12 1/12 1/12 1/12

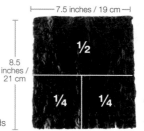

Nose — 4 triangles using a straw (medium)

Whiskers — 24 strands

Eyelashes — 24 strands

Cut extremely thin eyelashes out from the remaining nori sheet snippets and cut the whiskers out of the soy sauce kelp.

Use a straw to punch the eyes out of the soy sauce kelp and the cheeks and nose out of the fish sausage.

Eyes — 8 ovals using a straw (medium)

Cheeks — 8 ovals using a straw (medium)

PREPARATION

Separate the vinegared rice into the various needed portions.

7.05 oz / 200 g

0.35 oz / 10 g x 4

0.35 oz / 10 g x 2

0.18 oz / 5 g x 2

1. Creating the body parts

Cut three sides off the fish sausage (thick) to create a triangular stick.

Place the sausage on the edge of a 1/4 size nori sheet and spread vinegared rice 0.35 oz / 10 g along its edge in a stick shape.

Wrap into a triangular roll. (Create two of these.)

Ears

Hair on the Top

Create a 4 inch long stick shape out of vinegared rice (white), 0.35 oz / 10 g, and cover it with a 1/12 nori sheet to create a roundish triangle.

Hands

Place vinegared rice (white), 0.35 oz / 10 g, in a stick shape on the 1/8 nori sheet, roll and cut it lengthwise in half.

Cut four sides off the fish sausage (thin) to create a rectangular stick and wrap three sides of it with a 1/12 size nori sheet. If using a thicker sausage or hotdog, use the sample photo above as reference and cut to match the size and shape as closely as possible.

Place vinegared rice (pink), 0.35 oz / 10 g, on the 1/12 size nori sheet in a stick shape and wrap into a triangular sushi roll. (Create two of these.)

Attach the triangular rolls onto the side of the sausage to create a ribbon.

Ribbon (top half)

Ribbon (bottom half)

Place vinegared rice (pink), 0.18 oz / 5 g, in the middle of a 1/12 nori sheet in a stick shape and fold over the nori from both sides to create a triangle. (Create two of these.)

2. Assemble and Roll

1

Attach the 1/2 nori sheet and the 1/4 nori sheet with rice and place vinegared rice (white), 7.05 oz / 200 g, in the middle of the nori in the shape of a 2.4 inch / 6 cm wide dome.

2

Stretch rice grains out on the nori sheet along the bottom edge of the vinegared rice dome (to create creases in **3** for the fur on both sides of the face).

3

Pinch the nori in every 0.12 inch / 3 mm to create three strands of fur on both sides of the face.

4

Create a dent in the middle using a chopstick, bury the ribbon (bottom half) into it and adjust the shape as needed.

5

Keep the sushi mat on the table and wrap the nori around the roll by flipping the sushi mat over.

6

Flip the other side over and wrap up the sushi roll.

3. Cutting and Finishing Touches

1

Flatten the sides of the sushi roll and adjust the shape of the cheeks and fur as needed.

2

Cut the sushi roll into four even slices, wiping the kitchen knife with a wet cloth after each cut.

3

Cut each of the ears, hands, ribbon (top half) and hair on the top into four pieces.

4

Place the ribbon (top half) on top of the ribbon (bottom half) and adjust the shape of the entire ribbon.

5

Place the ears on both sides with the white side facing the ribbon.

6

Attach the hair on the top and the hands.

7

Place the nose, eyes and cheeks on the face in that order.

8

Place three strands of whiskers below each cheek and three strands of eyelashes on top of the eyes.

CHANGE THE EXPRESSION!!
★★★★★★★★★★★★★★★★
Marie seems so happy that you can almost hear her hum!

Cinderella

Cinderella is known for her blond hair and light blue headband.
Make her look even cuter by using longer eyelashes.

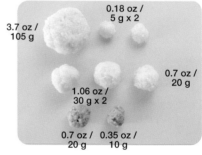

INGREDIENTS FOR FOUR SLICES

Vinegared Rice

Vinegared Rice (Light Peach), 4.05 oz / 115 g
(Vinegared rice 4.05 oz / 115 g + Deco Furi (pink), 1 pack)

Vinegared Rice (Yellow), 2.82 oz / 80 g
(Vinegared rice 2.82 oz / 80 g + a dash of pumpkin powder)

Vinegared Rice (Blue), 1.06 oz / 30 g
(Vinegared rice 0.9 oz / 25 g + Deco Furi (sky), 2 packs)

Ingredients

Kelp cooked in sweet soy sauce, 1 slice (eyes)

Fish sausage (thin slice), small amount (nose)

Nori Sheets

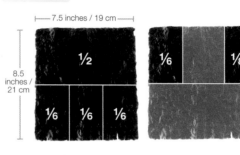

PREPARATION

Separate the vinegared rice into the various needed portions.

Eyes
8 ovals using a
straw (medium)

Squeeze the straw slightly to punch out
the eyes from the soy sauce kelp and the
nose from the fish sausage.

Nose 4 ovals using a
straw (medium)

Eyelashes 24 strands

Cut extremely thin
eyelashes out of the
remaining nori sheet
snippets.

Attention! The blue rice which has
been sandwiched by the
nori sheet will become the
hairband, so remember to
spread it out thoroughly.

1. Creating the body parts

Hands

Place vinegared rice (blue), 0.35 oz / 10 g, in a stick shape on the
1/8 nori sheet, roll and cut it lengthwise in half.

Hairband

Spread vinegared rice (blue), 0.7
oz / 20 g, evenly over a 1/6 size
nori sheet.

Place a 1/6 nori sheet over it and spread vinegared rice (yellow), 0.7
oz / 20 g, thoroughly on top of that nori sheet too.

Hair

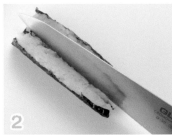

1 Place vinegared rice (yellow), 1.06 oz / 30 g, in a stick shape, on the 1/6 nori sheet and wrap it into a sushi roll. (Create two of these.)

2 Cut one of the rolls lengthwise in half. Cut the other roll in half too but be careful not to cut through the nori at the bottom.

3 Place the semi-cut sushi roll and half of the sushi roll side by side and place 0.18 oz / 5 g of vinegared rice (light peach) on each of the two dents.

4 The hair bun (left) and the front of her hair (right) are now complete.

2. Assemble and Roll

1 Place the sushi mat sideways on the table. Place a 1/2 nori sheet on the mat and put 3.7 oz / 105 g of vinegared rice (light peach), in a 1.6 inches / 4 cm wide stick shape, in the middle of the nori sheet.

2 Hold the sushi mat up in a U shape and place the front hair on the roll.

3 Place the hairband on the roll with the yellow side facing up.

Attention!

Before wrapping the roll, check from the front of the sushi roll if the front hair and hairband are in the correct position.

4 Wrap one side of the nori onto the rice.

5 Wrap the other side over to complete the sushi roll.

3. Cutting and Finishing Touches

1 Align the sushi roll with the edge of the sushi mat, gently wrap to adjust the shape of the roll and pat each side to flatten.

2 Cut the sushi roll into four even slices, wiping the kitchen knife with a wet cloth after each cut.

3 Cut the hair bun into four pieces, attach them on the face and adjust the details of the front hair using a bamboo skewer.

4 Cut each of the rolls for the hands into four pieces and attach them to the face.

5 Place the nose and eyes in that order.

6 Place three strands of eyelashes on each eye.

Snow White

DIFFICULTY 2
♥ ♥ ♡

Snow White's bangs and face are wrapped in the same roll. The hair under her ears and her ribbon are attached later.

actual size

Cheeks 8 ovals using a straw (medium)

Eyes 8 circles using a straw (medium)

Nose 4 ovals using a straw (medium)

Use a straw to punch the eyes out of the soy sauce kelp, the nose out of the cheese, and the cheeks out of the fish sausage.

Eyelashes 24 strands

Cut extremely thin eyelashes out from the remaining nori sheet snippets.

INGREDIENTS FOR FOUR SLICES

Vinegared Rice

Vinegared Rice (Light Peach), 5.3 oz / 150 g
(Vinegared rice 5.3 oz / 150 g + Deco Furi (pink), 1 pack)

Vinegared Rice (Black), 3.2 oz / 90 g
(Vinegared rice 2.82 oz / 80 g + ground black sesame 0.35 oz / 10 g + a dash of purple shiso seasoning)

Vinegared Rice (Red), 1.06 oz / 30 g
(Vinegared rice 1.06 oz / 30 g + Deco Furi (red), 1 pack)

Ingredients

Pickled burdock root (4 inches / 10 cm), 1 (center of the ribbon)

Kelp cooked in sweet soy sauce, 1 slice (eyes)

American cheese, 1/4 slice (nose)

Fish sausage, 0.8–1.2 inches / 2–3 cm (cheeks)

Nori Sheets

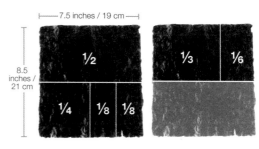

← 7.5 inches / 19 cm →

8.5 inches / 21 cm

½   ⅓   ⅙
¼ ⅛ ⅛

PREPARATION

Separate the vinegared rice into the various needed portions.

4.6 oz / 130 g
0.35 oz / 10 g x 2
1.06 oz / 30 g
1.06 oz / 30 g
0.7 oz / 20 g x 3

1. Creating the body parts

Ears
Hands

Place vinegared rice (light peach), 0.35 oz / 10 g, in a stick shape on the 1/8 nori sheet, wrap it into a roll (create two of these) and cut them lengthwise in half.

Ribbon

Place vinegared rice (white) 1.06 oz / 30 g, in a stick shape on the 1/4 nori sheet, roll and cut it lengthwise in half.

Hair

Place vinegared rice (black), 0.7 oz / 20 g, in a stick shape on the 1/6 nori sheet, roll and cut it lengthwise in half.

2. Assemble and Roll

1

Place the sushi mat sideways and place a 1/2 nori sheet on it. Spread 4.6 oz / 130 g of vinegared rice (light peach) in the middle of the nori in a mound that is 1.6 inches / 4 cm wide.

2

Place a 1/3 size nori sheet, which will be the borderline of the face and hair on the mound of rice and fold it to clarify the line of the front hair.

3

Spread 0.7 oz / 20 g of vinegared rice (black) 0.7 oz / 20 g along each side and spread them out so that they are flat.

4

Place 1.06 oz / 30 g of vinegared rice on the top, fold over the nori on the side and adjust the shape of the roll as needed.

5

Keep the sushi mat on the table and wrap the nori around the roll by flipping the sushi mat over.

6

Flip the remaining side over to complete the roll.

3. Cutting and Finishing Touches

1

Align the sushi roll with the edge of the sushi mat, gently wrap to adjust the shape of the roll and pat the side to flatten it.

2

Cut the sushi roll into four even slices, wiping the kitchen knife with a wet cloth after each cut.

3

Push the sushi roll from the top and bottom to fix any distortions in the face and adjust its shape as needed.

4

Cut the ears, hands, hair, and ribbon rolls into four equal pieces.

5

Cut the pickled burdock root into the same length as the ribbon, and attach the pieces together on the top of the face to create the ribbon.

6

Place the ears, hair, and hands in that order.

7

Place the nose, eyes, and cheek in that order.

8

Place the eyelashes on the face so they will overlap the eyes a bit.

CHANGE THE EXPRESSION!!
★★★★★★★★★★★★★★★★★
Sleeping Snow White.

Tinker Bell

Tinker Bell's bun hairstyle has bangs that are not symmetrical, so cut the roll using the method that will allow you to cut all the faces facing the same way.

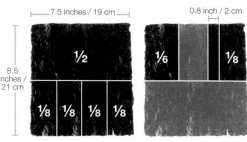

DIFFICULTY 3
♥ ♥ ♥

actual size

CHANGE THE EXPRESSION!!

A charming wink.

Use a straw to punch out the eyes out of the soy sauce kelp, the nose from the slice of cheese, and the cheek from the fish sausage.

Eyes 8 ovals using a straw (medium)

Cheeks 8 ovals using a straw (medium)

Nose 4 ovals using a straw (medium)

Eyelashes 24 strands

Cut extremely thin eyelashes out from the remaining nori sheet snippets.

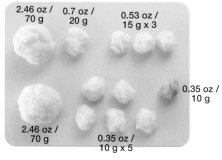
1. Creating the body parts

Ears
Hands

Place vinegared rice (light peach), 0.35 oz / 10 g, in a stick shape on the 1/8 nori sheet, wrap it into a roll (create two of these) and cut them lengthwise in half.

Bun

Spread vinegared rice (blue), 0.35 oz / 10 g, on top of the 0.8 inch / 2 cm strip of nori.

Flip the nori over and spread vinegared rice (yellow), 0.7 oz / 20 g, on top of it.

Place it in the middle of a 1/6 size nori sheet with the yellow side facing down and wrap it into a sushi roll. The yellow side is the bun, so it should be rounded and the blue side should be flattened.

 ← Bangs

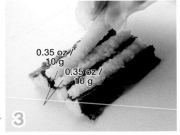

1 Create a 4 inch / 10 cm long triangular mound out of vinegared rice (yellow), 0.53 oz / 15 g. Fold a 1/8 nori sheet in half and cover the rice with it.

2 Create three of those, place them side by side, and overlap the remaining nori on top of one another.

Attention!
Pinch in the overlapping nori to connect the three triangular mounds together.

3 Place a stick of vinegared rice (light peach), 0.35 oz / 10 g, on one of the dents, and place two sticks of the same 0.35 oz / 10 g amount of rice on the other.

2. Assemble and Roll

1 Place the sushi mat sideways on the table. Place a 1/2 nori sheet on the mat and put 2.46 oz / 70 g of vinegared rice (light peach), in a 4 cm wide stick shape, in the middle of the nori sheet.

2 Hold the sushi mat up in a U shape and place the bangs on the roll.

3 Cover the roll with 2.46 oz / 70 g of vinegared rice (yellow) and form the rice into a dome shape.

4 Check if the decoration looks correct from the front of the roll and flip over each side of the sushi mat to wrap the sushi roll.

3. Cutting and Finishing Touches

1 Align the sushi roll with the edge of the sushi mat, gently wrap to adjust the shape of the roll, and pat the side to flatten it.

2 Cut the edge off slightly and then cut the roll into four equal slices.

Attention!
Cut a thin slice off the front end of the roll with the correct decoration showing, and then cut the roll into four equal slices for sushi rolls with decorations that are not symmetrical.

3 Cut each roll of the ears, hands and bun into four pieces.

4 Place the nose, eyes, cheeks, and eyelashes on the face in that order.

Attention!
Use the bun and nose to determine the center of the face when attaching the facial features on the face.

71

Anna

♥ ♥ ♥

Anna's bangs are wrapped into her face roll and her braids are actually attached to her face before they are all wrapped tightly with the sushi mat. Don't forget to add the lighter streak to her hair!

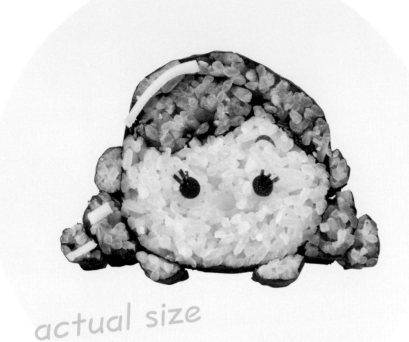

actual size

INGREDIENTS FOR FOUR SLICES

Vinegared Rice

Vinegared Rice (Light Peach), 5.64 oz / 160 g
(Vinegared rice 5.64 oz / 160 g + Deco Furi (pink) 1 pack)

Vinegared Rice (Brown), 3.9 oz / 110 g
(Vinegared rice 3.5 oz / 100 g + bonito rice seasoning 0.35 g / 10 g)

Ingredients

American cheese,1/2 slice (white streak in her hair)

Kelp cooked in sweet soy sauce, 1 slice (eyes, eyebrows)

Fish sausage (thin slice), small amount (nose)

Nori Sheets

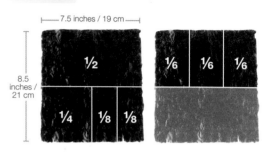

← 7.5 inches / 19 cm →

8.5 inches / 21 cm

| 1/2 | 1/6 | 1/6 | 1/6 |
| 1/4 | 1/8 | 1/8 | |

PREPARATION

Separate the vinegared rice into the various needed portions.

4.94 oz / 140 g

0.35 oz / 10 g x 2

1.23 oz / 35 g x 2

0.7 oz / 20 g x 2

Use a straw to punch the eyes and eyebrows out of the soy sauce kelp and the nose out of the fish sausage.

Nose 4 ovals using a straw (medium)

Eyes 8 circles using a straw (medium)

Eyebrows 4 strands

Punch out a circle with a straw (medium) and use the straw again to punch out a nicely shaped arc.

Mesh (Long) 4 strands

Mesh (Short) 8 strands

Cut the strips out of the cheese slice with a bamboo skewer.

1. Creating the body parts

Ears

Hands

Place vinegared rice (light peach), 0.35 oz /10 g, in a stick shape on the 1/8 nori sheet, wrap it into a roll (create two of these) and cut them lengthwise in half.

Bangs

Spread vinegared rice (brown), 1.23 oz / 35 g, over the 1/4 size nori sheet leaving 0.4 inch / 1 cm open on the right side open and fold the nori over once from the left side. Fold the nori over once from the right side too and create a shape that looks like this photo.

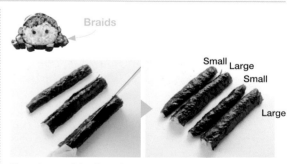

Braids

Small Large Small Large

Place vinegared rice (brown), 0.7 oz / 20 g, in a stick shape on the 1/6 nori sheet, wrap it into a roll (create two of these) and cut them lengthwise into a large half and small half.

2. Assemble, Roll and Assemble again

1 Place a 2 inch / 5 cm wide mound of vinegared rice (light peach), 4.94 oz / 140 g, in the middle of the 1/2 size nori sheet and pinch the top and shape the rice so the bangs can fit in on top.

2 Place the bangs so that they sit from the center to the left side of the rice.

3 Fold a 1/6 size nori sheet in half and place it on the right side for the dividing line of her hair.

Spread some rice on the nori to use as glue and fold the nori in half.

4 Cover the top with vinegared rice (brown), 1.23 oz / 35 g, and form the rice into a dome shape.

5 Keep the sushi mat on the table and wrap the nori around the roll by flipping each side of the sushi mat over.

6 With the top of the head facing down, shape the sushi roll and flatten the sides.

Ear
Big
Small

7 Attach the ear, large braid and small braid to each side of the face in that order.

Attention!
If you let the roll rest for a few minutes, the nori will get moist and will stick to each other.

3. Cutting and Finishing Touches

1 Align the sushi roll with the edge of the sushi mat, gently wrap to adjust the shape of the roll and pat the sides to flatten.

2 Cut a small slice off the edge and then cut into four equal slices. (→ p. 70, how to cut the Tinker Bell sushi roll.)

3 Cut the hands into four pieces and attach two onto each face.

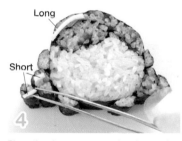

Long
Short

4 Place the cheese representing the mesh on the top of the head and on the braids.

5 Place the nose, eyes and eyebrows onto the face in that order.

6 Attach three strands of eyelashes on each eye.

CHANGE THE EXPRESSION!!
★★★★★★★★★★★★
Add freckles with ground sesame.

73

Elsa

Elsa has lovely hair. Wait for the sushi roll to moisten a bit after attaching her ears and hair before cutting.

actual size

INGREDIENTS FOR FOUR SLICES

Vinegared Rice

Vinegared Rice (Light Peach), 5.64 oz / 160 g
(Vinegared rice 5.64 oz / 160 g + a dash of ground white sesame)

Vinegared Rice (Yellow), 3.9 oz / 110 g
(Vinegared rice 3.9 oz / 110 g + a dash of pumpkin powder)

Ingredients

American cheese, 1/2 slice (tiara)

Kamaboko fish cake (thin slice), 1 slice
(jewel on her tiara, hair accessory)

Kelp cooked in sweet soy sauce, 1 slice (eyes, eyebrows)

Fish sausage (thin slice), Small amount (nose)

Nori Sheets

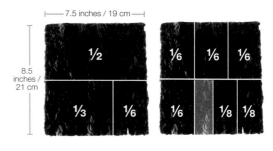

├─ 7.5 inches / 19 cm ─┤

8.5 inches / 21 cm

| 1/2 | 1/6 | 1/6 | 1/6 |
| 1/3 | 1/6 | 1/6 | 1/8 | 1/8 |

PREPARATION

Separate the vinegared rice into the various needed portions.

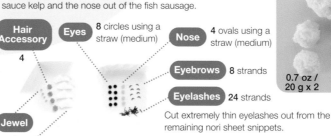

4.94 oz / 140 g

0.35 oz / 10 g x 2

0.7 oz / 20 g x 2

0.53 oz / 15 g x 2

Separate 1.4 oz / 40 g into three

Dilute the dye with water before use.

It will be easy if you use a flower-shaped cutter.

Cut the fish cake and then dye blue.

Use a straw to punch the eyes and eyebrows out of the soy sauce kelp and the nose out of the fish sausage.

Hair Accessory 4

Jewel 4

Eyes 8 circles using a straw (medium)

Nose 4 ovals using a straw (medium)

Eyebrows 8 strands

Eyelashes 24 strands

Cut extremely thin eyelashes out from the remaining nori sheet snippets.

Tiara 4 Cut the tiara out of the American cheese using a bamboo skewer.

CHANGE THE EXPRESSION!!

She will look even more charming when winking.

1. Creating the body parts

Ears

Hands

Ear

Hand

Place vinegared rice (light peach), 0.35 oz / 10 g, in a stick shape on the 1/8 nori sheet, wrap it into a roll (create two of these) and cut them lengthwise in half.

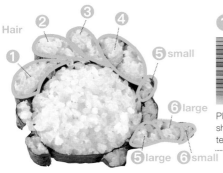

Hair ① ② ③ ④
⑤ small
⑥ large
⑤ large ⑥ small

① ② ③ ④ ⑤ large ⑥ large

⑤ small ⑥ small

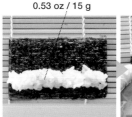

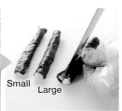

⑤ large ⑤ small ⑥ large ⑥ small

0.53 oz / 15 g

Place vinegared rice (yellow), 0.53 oz / 15 g, in a stick shape, on a 1/6 size nori sheet and wrap into sushi roll. (Create two of these.)

Cut each one lengthwise into a large half and small half.

Small Large

① ② 0.7 oz / 20 g

Place vinegared rice (yellow), 0.7 oz / 20 g, in a stick shape, on a 1/6 size nori sheet and wrap into a teardrop-shaped roll. (Create two of these.)

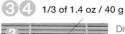 ③ ④ 1/3 of 1.4 oz / 40 g

Divide the vinegared rice (yellow) 1.4 oz / 40 g into three portions.

③ Wrap 1/3 of the vinegared rice into a teardrop shape with a 1/6 nori sheet.

④ Place 1/3 of the vinegared rice on a 1/3 size nori sheet and wrap once, add the remaining 1/3 to the roll and wrap up the sushi roll.

1/3 of 1.4 oz / 40 g

1/3 of 1.4 oz / 40 g

---

2. Assemble and Roll

① Place vinegared rice (light peach), 4.94 oz / 140 g, at the bottom of the 1/2 nori sheet at a width of 2.4 inches / 6 cm and wrap into a round sushi roll.

② Align the sushi roll with the edge of the sushi mat, gently wrap to adjust the shape of the roll and pat the sides to flatten.

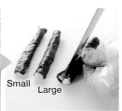

③ Stretch rice onto the roll as glue and attach hair ① onto the roll.

④ Attach ②, ③, ④, ⑤ small tightly next to each other to the roll in order.

⑤ Attach the left and right ear.
Ear   Ear

⑥ Attach ⑤ large, ⑥ large and ⑥ small together and then place on the bottom right side of ⑤. Let the sushi roll rest for a while so the nori will moisten and stick together.

---

3. Cutting and Finishing Touches

① Adjust the shape of the entire roll and flatten the sides. Cut a small slice off the edge and then cut into four equal slices. (→ See p. 70, how to cut the Tinker Bell sushi roll.)

② Cut the hands into four pieces and attach two onto each face.

③ Place the nose, eyes, eyebrows, and eyelashes in that order.

④ Place the tiara, jewel, and hair accessory.

Olaf

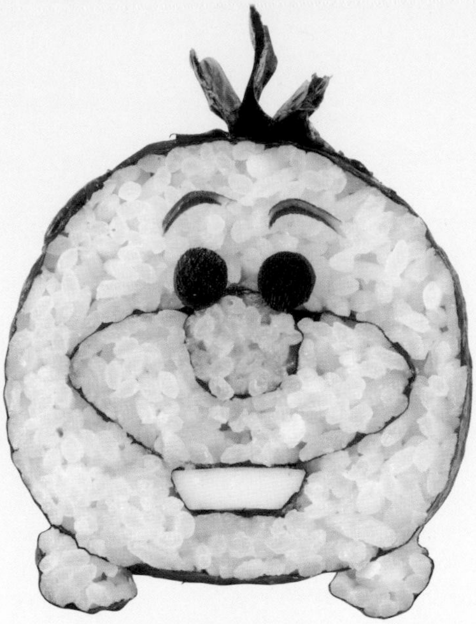
actual size

Simply position the orange nose and cheese teeth in the center and you've got yourself an Olaf!

DIFFICULTY 1

INGREDIENTS FOR FOUR SLICES

Vinegared Rice

Vinegared Rice (White), 7.76 oz / 220 g

Vinegared Rice (Orange), 0.53 oz / 15 g
(Vinegared rice 0.53 oz / 15 g + a dash of Deco Furi (orange))

Ingredients

Hard white cheese, 1 piece (teeth)

Kelp cooked in sweet soy sauce, 2 slices (eyes, eyebrows)

Nori Sheets

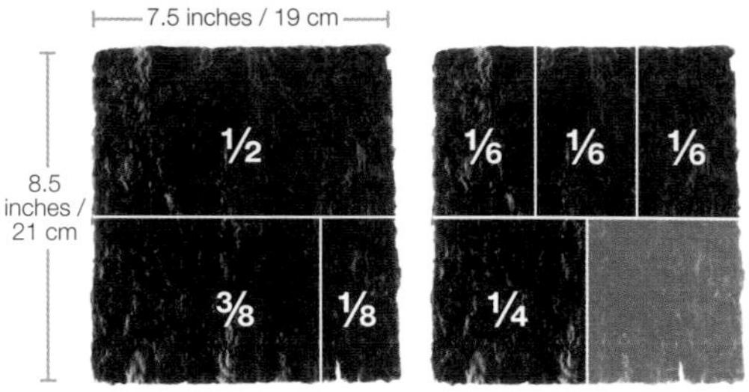
7.5 inches / 19 cm
8.5 inches / 21 cm
½
⅜
⅛
⅙
⅙
⅙
¼

PREPARATION

Separate the vinegared rice into the various needed portions.

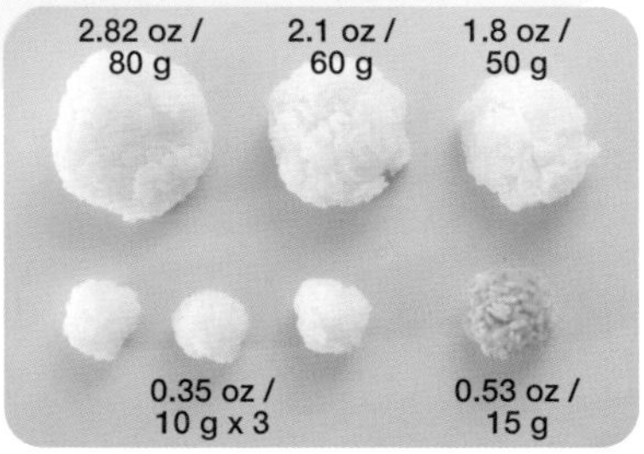
2.82 oz / 80 g
2.1 oz / 60 g
1.8 oz / 50 g
0.35 oz / 10 g x 3
0.53 oz / 15 g

Use a straw to punch the eyes and eyebrows out of the soy sauce kelp.

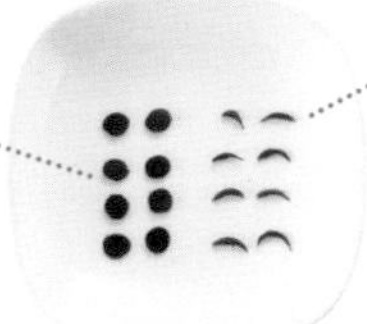

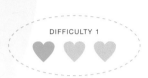

Eyes 8 circles using a straw (wide)

Eyebrows 8 strands

Punch out a circle with a straw (wide) and use the straw again to punch out a nicely shaped arc.

1. Creating the body parts

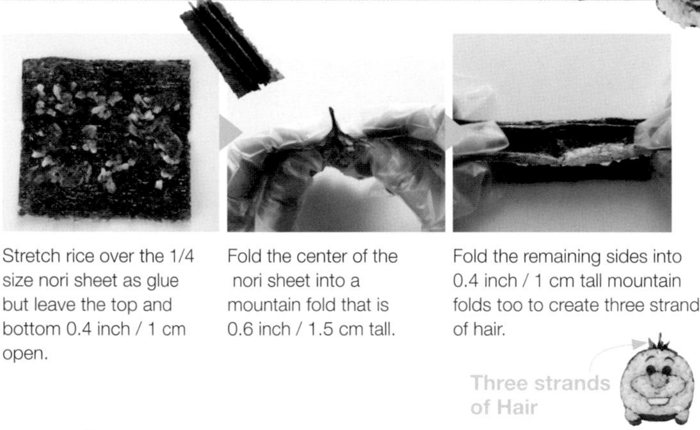
Three strands of Hair

Stretch rice over the 1/4 size nori sheet as glue but leave the top and bottom 0.4 inch / 1 cm open.

Fold the center of the nori sheet into a mountain fold that is 0.6 inch / 1.5 cm tall.

Fold the remaining sides into 0.4 inch / 1 cm tall mountain folds too to create three strands of hair.

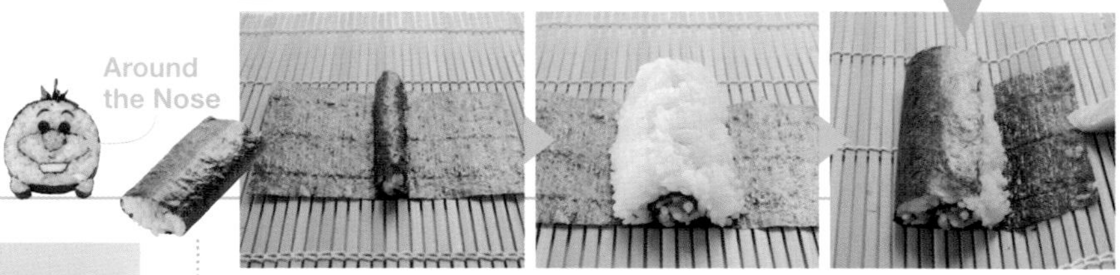
Around the Nose
Attention!
Create a flat oval with thin edges.

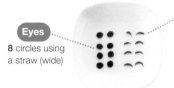

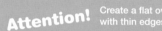

Place the nose in the center of the 3/8 size nori sheet.

Cover the nose with a 2 inch / 5 cm wide heap of vinegared rice (white) 2.1 oz / 60 g to create the oval shape.

Wrap the nori over from each side.

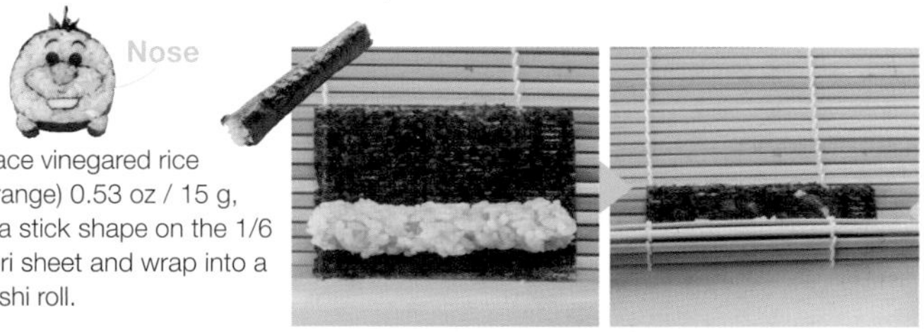
Nose

Place vinegared rice (orange) 0.53 oz / 15 g, in a stick shape on the 1/6 nori sheet and wrap into a sushi roll.

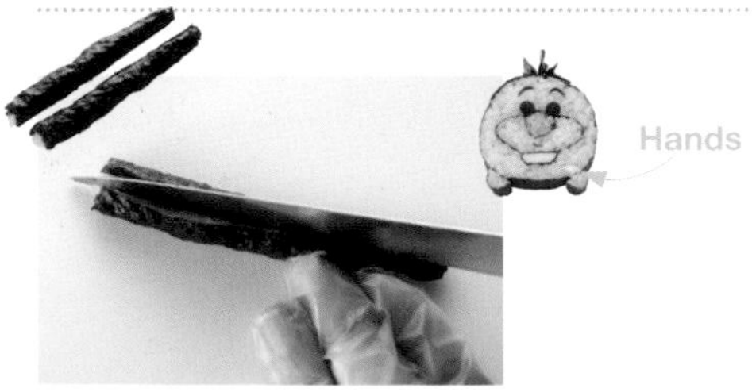
Hands

Place a vinegared rice (white), 0.35 oz / 10 g, in a stick shape on the 1/8 nori sheet, wrap it into a roll and cut them lengthwise into halves.

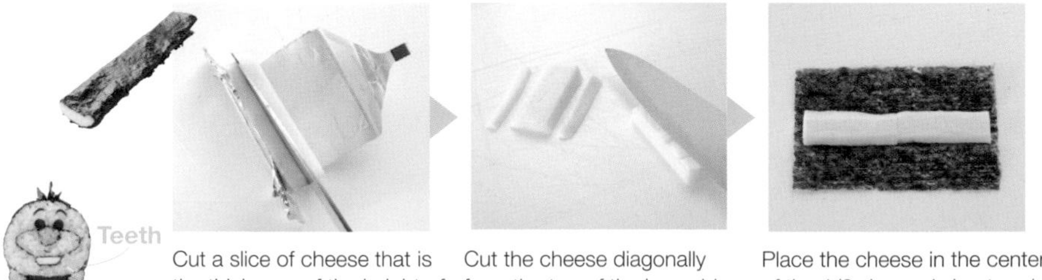
Teeth

Cut a slice of cheese that is the thickness of the height of Olaf's teeth. Use the sample image above as reference.

Cut the cheese diagonally from the top of the long side to create a trapezoid. (If using cheese less than 4 inches, cut two of these.)

Place the cheese in the center of the 1/6 size nori sheet and wrap the nori over from the closer side, followed by the farther side.

2. Assemble and Roll

1 Connect the 1/2 and 1/6 size nori sheet together and spread vinegared rice (white) 1.8 oz / 50 g in the middle of the nori so that it is 4.7 inches / 12 cm wide.

2 Place the teeth on the rice with the narrow side facing down and line both sides of the teeth with 0.35 oz / 10 g of vinegared rice.

3 Place the nose sushi roll on top with the orange nose facing up.

4 Cover it with a heap of vinegared rice 2.82 oz / 80 g.

5 Keep the sushi mat on the table and wrap the nori around the roll by flipping each side of the sushi mat over.

6 Wrap the nori on top of each other to complete the sushi roll.

3. Cutting and Finishing Touches

1 Align the sushi roll with the edge of the sushi mat, gently wrap to adjust the shape of the roll and pat the sides to flatten.

2 Cut the sushi roll into four even slices, wiping the kitchen knife with a wet cloth after each cut.

3 Cut the three strands of hair and each of the hands into four pieces and attach to the face.

4 Please the eyes and eyebrows on the face in that order.

CHANGE THE EXPRESSION!!
★★★★★★★★★★★★★★★★
Cheerful singing Olaf.

77

Little Green Men

DIFFICULTY 2

Wrap cheese sticks in green vinegared rice to create the three eyes. Attach the antenna on the top and the pointed ears on the sides and you're done!

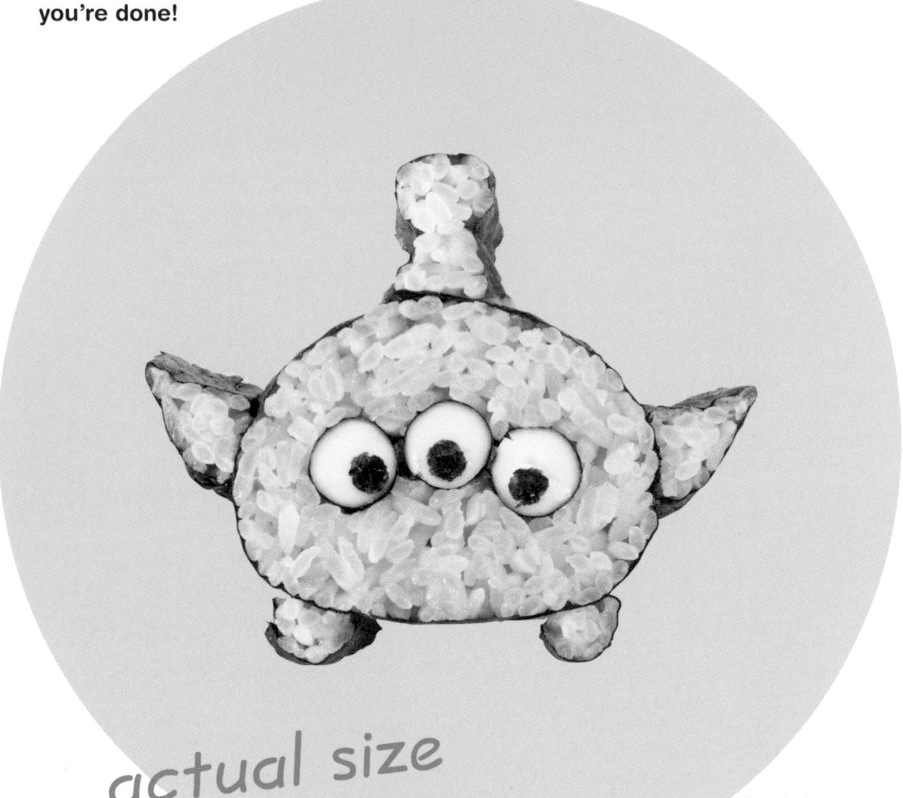
actual size

INGREDIENTS FOR FOUR SLICES

Vinegared Rice

Vinegared Rice (Green), 7.76 oz / 220 g
(Vinegared rice 7.4 oz / 210 g + Deco Furi (green) 0.35 oz / 10 g)

Ingredients

Cheese stick (4 inches), 3 sticks (eyes)

Nori Sheets

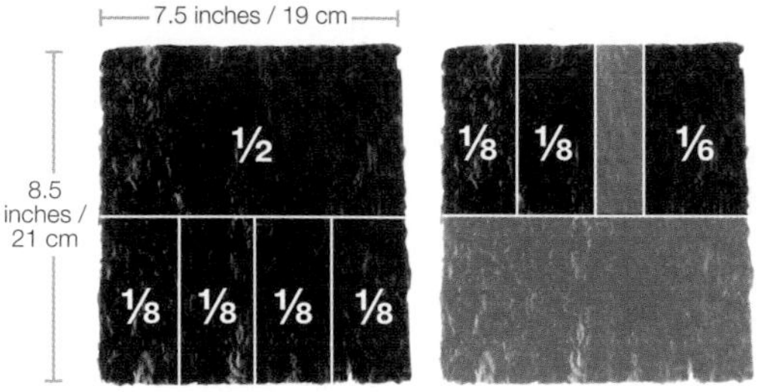
7.5 inches / 19 cm
8.5 inches / 21 cm
1/2
1/8
1/8
1/8
1/8
1/8
1/8
1/6

PREPARATION

Separate the vinegared rice into the various needed portions.

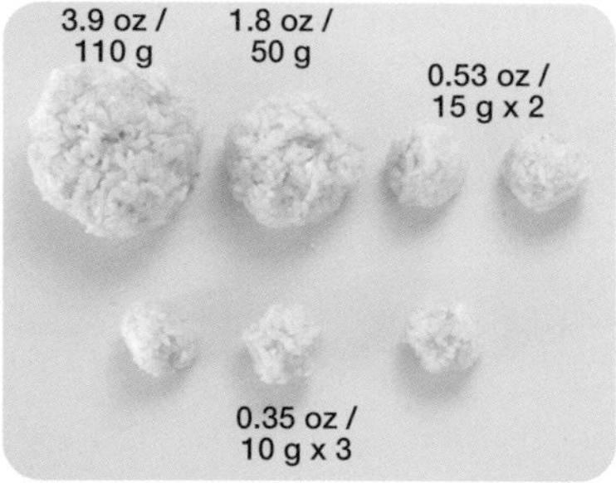
3.9 oz / 110 g
1.8 oz / 50 g
0.53 oz / 15 g x 2
0.35 oz / 10 g x 3

Possible Substitute Ideas

Another option is to make the face completely solid green, and then punch out cheese circles for each of the eyes. The benefit is that you get cleaner looking eyes, but you don't get the little black outline. To do this, you would need the main face to have an extra 30 g of rice (so it would be 140 g), and then you would skip steps 2 and 3. Then you punch out eyes from American cheese using an extra wide straw.

Punch the eyes out of the nori snippets using a nori sheet puncher.

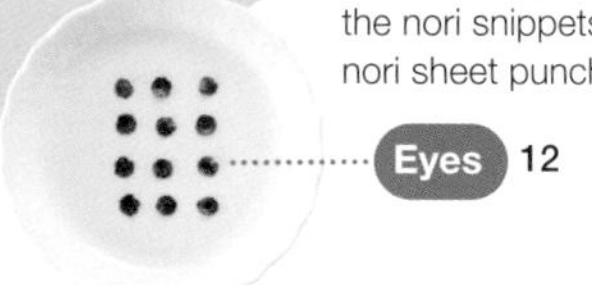
Eyes 12

1. Creating the body parts

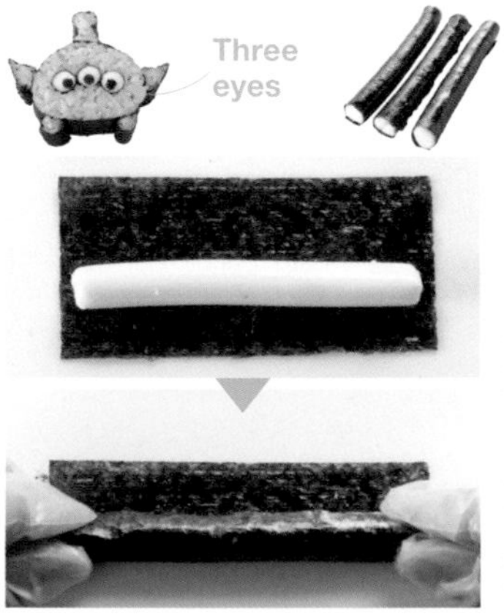
Three eyes

Wrap each cheese stick with a 1/8 nori sheet. (Create three of them.)

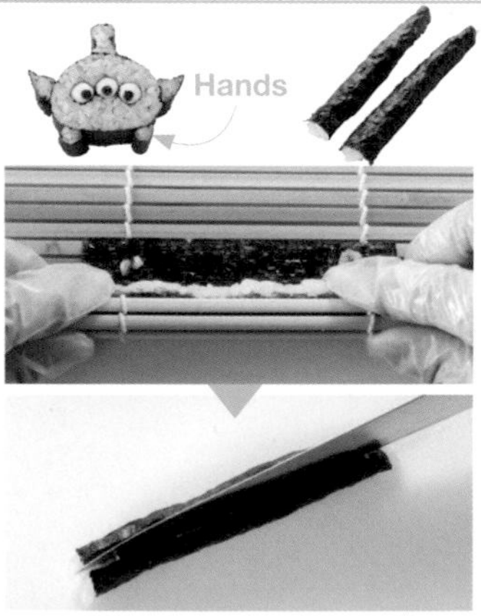
Hands

Place vinegared rice (green) 0.35 oz / 10 g on the 1/8 nori sheet, roll and cut it lengthwise in half.

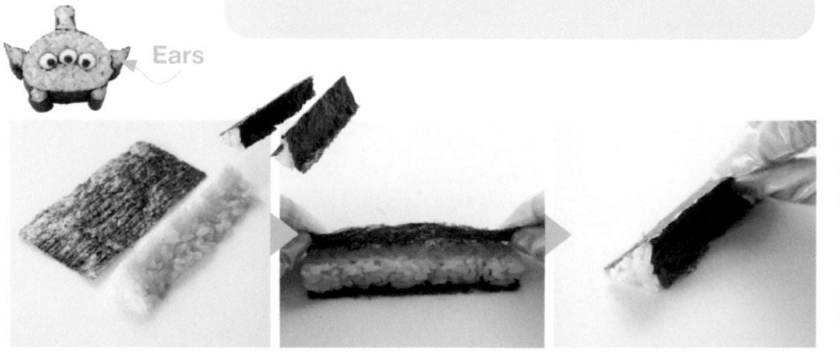
Ears

Use 0.53 oz / 15 g of vinegared rice to create a 4 inches / 10 cm long triangular mound that resembles the ear.

Wrap its side with a 1/8 size nori sheet. (Create two of these.)

Make the tip pointed and adjust the shape of the ear.

Antenna

1 Use 0.35 oz / 10 g of vinegared rice to create a 4 inches / 10 cm long stick and another 0.35 oz / 10 g to create a triangular stick.

2 Place the stick in the middle of the 1/6 size nori sheet.

3 Lightly pinch in from both sides to moisten the nori.

4 Place the triangular stick on top of 3 with the pointed side facing down and adjust the shape of the senor.

2. Assemble and Roll

1 Place a round mound of 1.8 oz / 50 g of vinegared rice that is 2 inches / 5 cm wide in the middle of a 1/2 nori sheet.

2 Place one eye in the middle and place the other two eyes to either side along the contour of the rounded rice.

3 Cover all of it with 3.9 oz / 110 g of vinegared rice and shape it into a dome.

4 Keep the sushi mat on the table and wrap the nori around the roll by flipping each side of the sushi mat over.

3. Cutting and Finishing Touches

1 Align the sushi roll with the edge of the sushi mat, gently wrap to adjust the shape of the roll and pat each side to flatten.

2 Cut the sushi roll into four even slices, wiping the kitchen knife with a wet cloth after each cut.

3 Cut each of the hands, ears and sensors into four equal pieces.

4 Place the sensor on the top of the head and attach the ears onto the sides paying attention to which direction the ears are pointing.

5 Attach the hands.

6 Place the nori eyes onto the face.

CHANGE THE EXPRESSION!!
★★★★★★★★★★★★★★★
Communicating with outer space?

Possible Substitute Ideas

If you want to try a workaround for the Little Green Men, instead of perfectly round cheese sticks, you could also make sushi rolls for each of the eyes and place nori on top. To do this, you'd need to create 3 sushi rolls that are the same size as the hands, using white rice (each roll will need 1/8 nori, plus 10 g rice).

Peas-in-a-Pod

Three peas in a pod. Place the eyebrows and eyes on the roll carefully so they have a well-balanced face.

DIFFICULTY 1
♥ ♥ ♥

actual size

Vinegared Rice

Vinegared Rice (Green), 4.2 oz / 120 g
(Vinegared rice 4.05 oz / 115 g + Deco Furi (green), 2 packs)

Vinegared Rice (Blue-Green), 3.5 oz / 100 g
(Vinegared rice 3.5 oz / 100 g + a dash of Deco Furi (green, sky))

Ingredients

Kelp cooked in sweet soy sauce, 1 slice (eyebrows, eyes)

Fish sausage (thin), 0.8–1.2 inches / 2–3 cm (mouth)

Nori Sheets

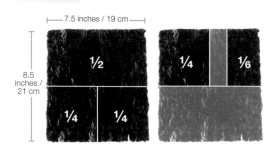

7.5 inches / 19 cm

8.5 inches / 21 cm

½ | ¼ | ⅙
¼ | ¼

PREPARATION

Separate the vinegared rice into the various needed portions.

2.46 oz / 70 g | 1.06 oz / 30 g

1.4 oz / 40 g x 3

Eyes **Eyebrows**

Cut the soy sauce kelp into thin strips for the eyes, and slightly thicker strips for the eyebrows.

Mouth 12

Cut the fish sausage into 0.08–0.12 inch / 2-3 mm thick slices and use a straw (medium) to punch out the mouth shapes you want.

1. Creating the body parts

Peas

Place vinegared rice (green) 1.4 oz / 40 g, in a stick shape, on the bottom of the 1/4 size nori sheet.

Roll into a sushi roll.

Create three rolls.

Attention!

You can create a nice round sushi roll by wrapping the completed roll in the sushi mat and rolling it up and down inside of the mat.

2. Assemble and Roll

1 Connect a 1/2 and 1/6 nori sheet together and place a 2.4 inches / 6 cm wide mound of vinegared rice (blue-green) 1.06 oz / 30 g in the center of the nori.

2 Place the three rolls for the peas right next to each other.

3 Cover the rolls with 2.46 oz / 70 g of vinegared rice (blue-green) which has been rounded at the top and adjust the shape of the rice.

4 Keep the sushi mat on the table and wrap the nori around the roll by flipping each side of the sushi mat over.

3. Cutting and Finishing Touches

1 Align the sushi roll with the edge of the sushi mat, gently wrap to adjust the shape of the roll and pat each side to flatten.

2 Cut the sushi roll into four even slices, wiping the kitchen knife with a wet cloth after each cut.

3 Choose the mouths that will give character to the peas and place them on each of the faces.

4 Cut the soy sauce kelp for the eyes into fine bits.

5 Place them on the faces carefully.

6 Cut the thin eyebrows using a bamboo skewer and place them on the face

CHANGE THE EXPRESSION!!
★★★★★★★★★★★★★★★★
It looks like they're talking loudly.

Lotso

Lotso's main features are his thick eyebrows and large round eyes. The light yellow area around his nose should be thicker on the bottom than at the top when rolled.

actual size

INGREDIENTS FOR FOUR SLICES

Vinegared Rice

Vinegared Rice (Purple), 6.35 oz / 180 g
(Vinegared rice 6.35 oz / 180 g + Deco Furi (purple), 1 pack)

Vinegared Rice (Light Yellow), 1.8 oz / 50 g
(Vinegared rice 1.8 oz / 50 g + a dash of Deco Furi (yellow))

Vinegared Rice (Dark Purple), 1.4 oz / 40 g
(Vinegared rice 40 g + a dash of purple sweet potato power and purple shiso seasoning)

Ingredients

Cheese stick (4 inches / 10 cm), 1 stick (ears)

Kelp cooked in sweet soy sauce, 3 slices (eyebrows, eyes)

Nori Sheets

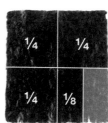

|← 7.5 inches / 19 cm →|

8.5 inches / 21 cm

1/2 · 3/8 · 1/8 · 1/4 · 1/4 · 1/4 · 1/8

PREPARATION

Separate the vinegared rice into the various needed portions.

2.82 oz / 80 g · 2.1 oz / 60 g · 0.53 oz / 15 g x 2 · 0.9 oz / 25 g x 2 · 1.4 oz / 40 g · 0.35 oz / 10 g

Use a straw to punch the eyebrows and eyes out of the soy sauce kelp.

 Eyes
8 circles using a straw (wide)

 Eyebrows
8 strands

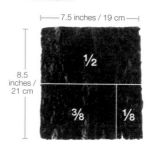

Punch a circle out and cut the top and bottom off with the straw (wide) to use the thickest piece in the middle as the thick eyebrow.

1. Creating the body parts

 Hands

 Nose

Ears

Place vinegared rice (purple) 0.35 oz / 10 g, in a stick shape on the 1/8 nori sheet, roll and cut it lengthwise in half.

Place a 1.2 inches / 3 cm wide mound of vinegared rice (dark purple) 1.4 oz / 40 g on the 1/4 size nori sheet and wrap into a triangular roll.

Cut the cheese stick lengthwise in half. Cut a 0.6 inch / 1.5 cm wide strip off the 1/4 nori sheet and cover the cheese with it. (Create two of these.)

Cover them with 0.53 oz / 15 g of vinegared rice (purple) in a dome shape.

Cover the rice with the remaining sheet of nori and fold any remaining nori sheet over to the bottom (the flat side).

82

Around the nose

1.

1 Spread 0.9 oz / 25 g of vinegared rice (yellow) over a width of 2.4 inches / 6 cm on a 3/8 size nori sheet but leave 0.4 inch / 1 cm at the bottom open.

2 Place the nose on the rice with the flat side facing down.

3 Cover it with a heap of vinegared rice (light yellow) 0.9 oz / 25 g.

4 Roll over to the far side into an oval.

Attention! The area above the nose should be flat and the area under the nose should be thick and rounded for this oval sushi roll.

2. Assemble and Roll

1 Connect 1/2 and 1/8 size nori sheet together, place it sideways, and spread 2.82 oz / 80 g of vinegared rice (purple) over it but leave 1.2 inches / 3 cm on both ends open.

2 Place the roll with the nose in the middle of the rice, with the flat side (the thin yellow side) facing up.

3 Place a heap of vinegared rice (purple) 2.1 oz / 60 g over it.

4 Keep the sushi mat on the table and wrap the nori around the roll by flipping each side of the sushi mat over.

3. Cutting and Finishing Touches

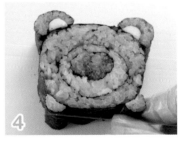

1 Align the sushi roll with the edge of the sushi mat, gently wrap to adjust the shape of the roll and pat each side to flatten.

2 Cut the sushi roll into four even slices, wiping the kitchen knife with a wet cloth after each cut.

3 Cut each roll of the ears and hands into four equal pieces.

4 Attach the ears and hands.

5 The eyes should be right near the nose.

6 Place the thick eyebrows on the face.

CHANGE THE EXPRESSION!!
****
Just move the eyebrows up and you get a scary looking face!

Sulley

Prepare by cutting the chikuwa (tube-shaped fish cake) and dying it. The rolling part is simple! Your Sulley will turn out great!

actual size

INGREDIENTS FOR FOUR SLICES

Vinegared Rice

Vinegared Rice (Blue), 7.76 oz / 220 g
(Vinegared rice 7.4 oz / 210 g + Deco Furi (sky) 0.35 g / 10 g)

Ingredients

Chikuwa, 1 (horns, eyebrows, nose)
Kelp cooked in sweet soy sauce, 1 slice (eyes)

Nori Sheets

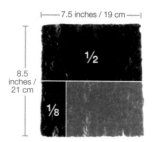

7.5 inches / 19 cm

8.5 inches / 21 cm

½

⅛

PREPARATION

Separate the vinegared rice into the various needed portions.

7.4 oz / 210 g

0.35 oz / 10 g

Chikuwa

Chikuwa is fish cake (surimi) that has been steamed or broiled after being wrapped around a stick. It ends up looking like a tube. The name "chikuwa" means "bamboo ring," which is what it resembles.

Use a straw to punch the eyebrows and eyes out of the soy sauce kelp.

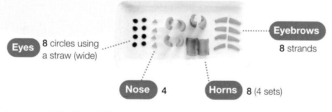

Eyes 8 circles using a straw (wide)

Nose 4

Horns 8 (4 sets)

Eyebrows 8 strands

Cut the chikuwa into the needed shapes and dye them blue using food dye.

Horns

Cut the chikuwa lengthwise in half and cut those halves into four pieces (8 pieces in all).

Cut the tip on one side diagonally, so the horn will be pointed.

Now you have horns that are sharp and pointy at the top. (1 set)

Eyebrows, Nose

Use the scraps from the horns and cut out thick eyebrows that are around 0.8 inch / 2 cm long and 0.2 inch / 5 mm sized noses.

Dilute the food dye before use.

1. Creating the body parts

Hands

Place vinegared rice 0.35 oz / 10 g, in a stick shape on the 1/8 nori sheet, roll and cut it lengthwise in half.

2. Roll

1 Place the sushi mat sideways. Place 7.4 oz / 210 g of vinegared rice in a stick shape, on a 1/2 sheet nori leaving 1.2 inches / 3 cm open from the bottom.

2 Lift the bottom of the sushi mat while holding the vinegared rice and roll to the far end of the sushi mat.

3 Pull the sushi mat over to you and roll tightly.

3. Cutting and Finishing Touches

1 Align the sushi roll with the edge of the sushi mat, gently wrap to adjust the shape of the roll and pat each side to flatten.

2 Cut the sushi roll into four even slices, wiping the kitchen knife with a wet cloth after each slice and then adjust the shape of the rolls into a clean-cut circle.

3 Cut each of the hands into four pieces and attach two onto the roll.

4 Attach the horns.

Attention!
The horns fall off easily, so use thin pieces of pasta (uncooked) to pin them into place and break off any unneeded pieces. The pasta will absorb the moisture and will naturally soften, so they are edible.

5 Place the eyes, eyebrows and nose on the face in that order.

You can also use a cucumber or bell pepper for the nose.

CHANGE THE EXPRESSION!!

Sulley with his mouth wide open. The sharp teeth are triangles cut out of a cheese slice.

Mike Wazowski

Mike's round black pupil has been double wrapped by white vinegared rice and green vinegared rice. The white rice grain will add a glint to his eye.

DIFFICULTY 1
♥ ♥ ♥

actual size

INGREDIENTS FOR FOUR SLICES

Vinegared Rice

Vinegared Rice (White), 2.46 oz / 70 g

Vinegared Rice (Green), 6 oz / 170 g
(Vinegared rice 5.64 oz / 160 g + Deco Furi (green) 0.35 oz / 10 g)

Vinegared Rice (Black), 0.53 oz/ 15 g
(Vinegared rice 0.53 oz / 15 g + ground black sesame)

Nori Sheets

← 7.5 inches / 19 cm →

8.5 inches / 21 cm

½ ⅛ 1/12 1/12

⅜ ⅛

PREPARATION

Separate the vinegared rice into the various needed portions.

4.94 oz / 140 g

0.35 oz / 10 g x 3

2.46 oz / 70 g

0.53 oz / 15 g

CHANGE THE EXPRESSION!!
You can almost hear him chatting away.

---

1. Creating the body parts

 Horns

 Pupil

 Hands

Create a 4 inches / 10 cm long mound out of 0.35 oz / 10 g of vinegared rice (green).

Fold the 1/12 nori sheet in half, cover the rice, and shape into a triangle. (Create two of these.)

Place vinegared rice (black) 0.53 oz / 15 g, in a stick shape, on the 1/8 nori sheet and wrap it into a sushi roll.

Place vinegared rice (green) 0.35 oz / 10 g, in a stick shape on the 1/8 nori sheet, roll and cut it lengthwise in half.

2. Assemble and Roll

1

Place a 3/8 size nori sheet upright on the mat and spread 2.46 oz / 70 g of vinegared rice (white) over it leaving 1.6 inches / 4 cm open at the top.

2

Place the pupil 1.2 inches / 3 cm above the bottom.

3

Lift up the bottom of the sushi mat facing you and roll it over.

4

The eye is complete.

Attention!
The trick is to make the rice in the middle area slightly thicker and the rice around the edge thinner.

5

Spread 4.94 oz / 140 g of vinegared rice (green) over the 1/2 nori sheet leaving 1.6 inches / 4 cm open at the top end.

6

Place the eye from 4 on top of the rice 1.2 inches / 3 cm above from the bottom.

7

Hold the sushi down as you lift the sushi mat up and roll away from yourself.

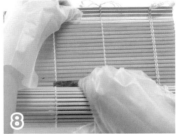

8

Pull the mat over to you as you wrap the roll up tightly.

3. Cutting and Finishing Touches

1

Align the sushi roll with the edge of the sushi mat, gently wrap to adjust the shape of the roll and pat the sides to flatten.

2

Cut the sushi roll into four even slices, wiping the kitchen knife with a wet cloth after each cut.

3

Cut each of the hands and horns into four pieces and attach them onto the face.

4

Split a rice grain apart with a bamboo skewer and place it on the pupil.

Baymax

Simple but super cute!!

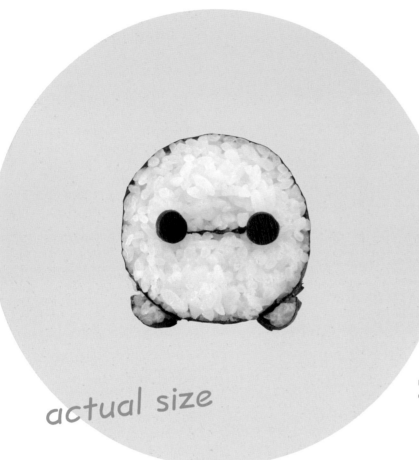

actual size

INGREDIENTS FOR FOUR SLICES

Vinegared Rice

Vinegared Rice (White), 7.76 oz / 220 g

Ingredients

Kelp cooked in sweet soy sauce, 2 slices (eyes)

Nori Sheets

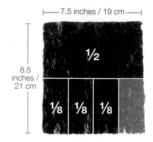

PREPARATION

Separate the vinegared rice into the various needed portions.

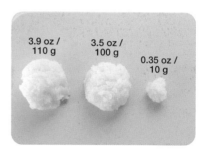

Use a straw to punch the eyes out of the soy sauce kelp.

Eyes 8 circles using a straw (extra wide)

Attention! Check from the front of the roll to be sure that the vinegared rice is shaped into a nice semicircle.

1. Creating the body parts

Hands

Place vinegared rice (white) 0.35 oz / 10 g, in a stick shape on the 1/8 nori sheet, roll and cut it lengthwise in half.

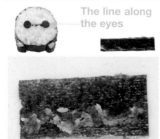

The line along the eyes

Stretch rice out on one half of the 1/8 sizes nori sheet, fold in half and glue it tightly together.

2. Assemble and Roll

Place the sushi mat sideways. Connect the 1/2 and 1/8 nori sheet together, place it on the mat and place 3.5 oz / 100 g of vinegared rice in the middle of the nori in a stick shape.

Place the sushi mat on your hand and hold it up in a U shape.

3 Place the black line between the eyes in the middle.

4 Place a heap of vinegared rice 3.9 oz / 110 g on top in a dome shape.

5 Wrap one side of the nori sheet with the sushi mat.

6 Flip the other side of the sushi mat over to wrap the nori around tightly.

3. Cutting and Finishing Touches

1 Align the sushi roll with the edge of the sushi mat, gently wrap to adjust the shape of the roll and pat each side to flatten.

2 Cut the sushi roll into four even slices, wiping the kitchen knife with a wet cloth after each cut.

3 Cut the hands into four pieces each and attach two onto the face.

4 Place the eyes on the ends of the black line.

Make a bunch and stack them up!

Baymax (Red)

Baymax is wearing red armor, so a black nori sheet has been sandwiched by the white fish cake to emphasize his eyes.

DIFFICULTY 2

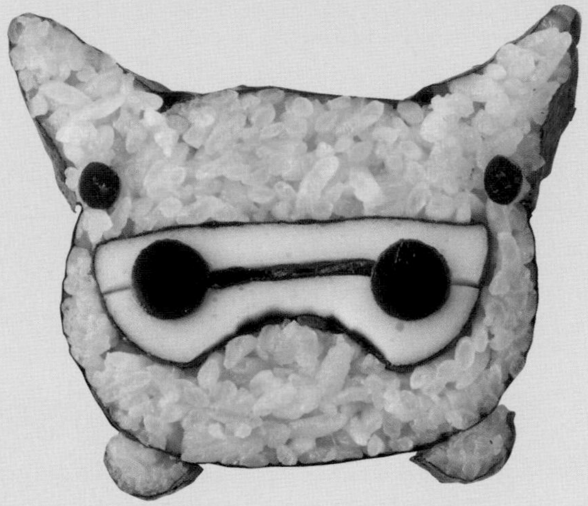

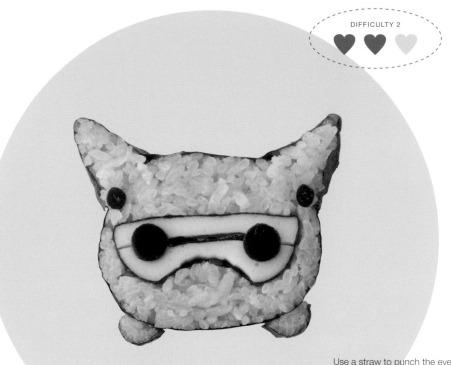

actual size

Use a straw to punch the eyes and decoration out of the soy sauce kelp.

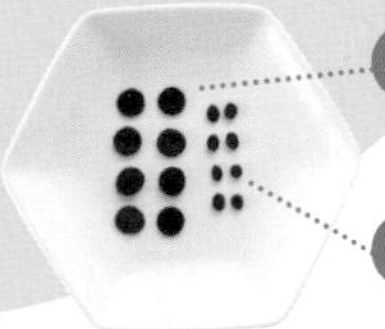

Eyes 8 circles using a straw (extra wide)

Decorations 8 ovals using a straw (medium)

INGREDIENTS FOR FOUR SLICES

Vinegared Rice

Vinegared Rice (Green), 6 oz / 170 g
(Vinegared rice 6.7 oz / 190 g + Deco Furi (orange) 0.35 oz / 10 g)

Ingredients

Kamaboko fish cake (white), 1 slice (area around the eyes)
Kelp cooked in sweet soy sauce, 3 slices (eyes, decorations)

Nori Sheets

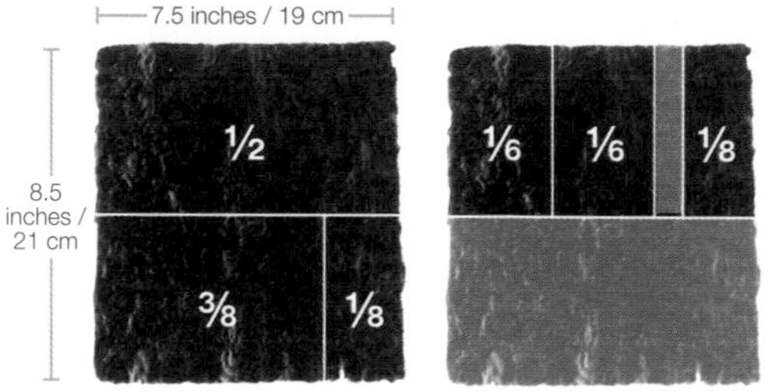
7.5 inches / 19 cm
8.5 inches / 21 cm
1/2
3/8
1/8
1/6
1/6
1/8

PREPARATION

Separate the vinegared rice into the various needed portions.

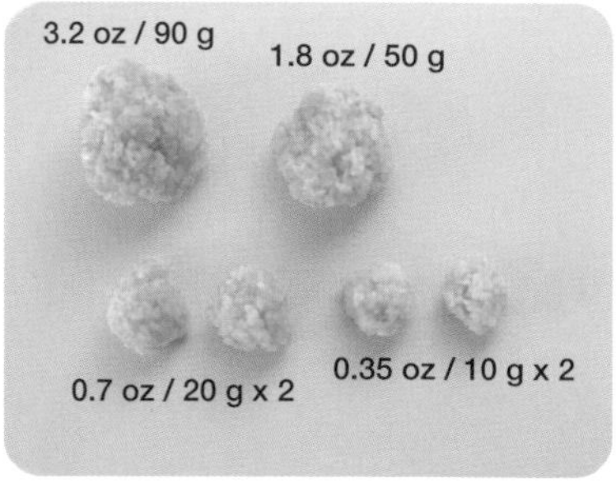
3.2 oz / 90 g
1.8 oz / 50 g
0.7 oz / 20 g x 2
0.35 oz / 10 g x 2

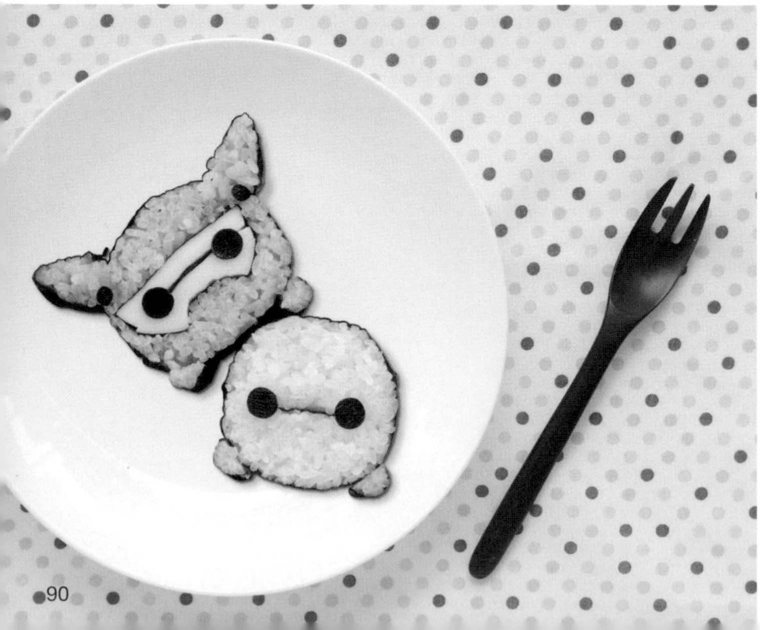

1. Creating the body parts

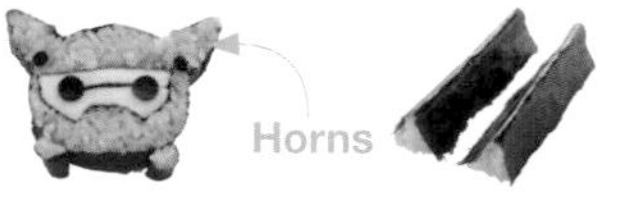
Horns

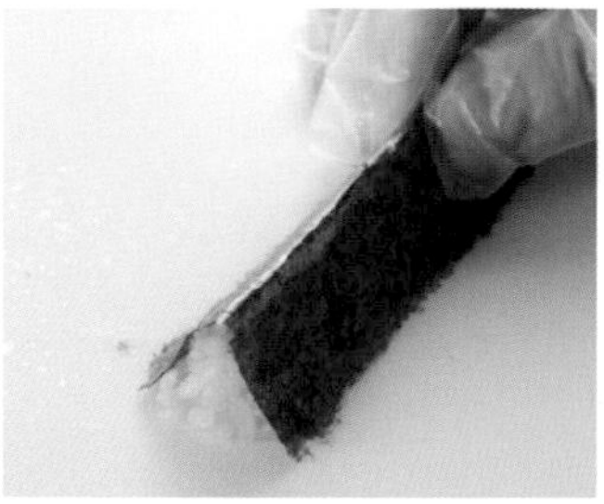

Create a 4 inch / 10 cm long mound out of 0.7 oz / 20 g of vinegared rice. Fold the 1/6 size nori sheet in half, cover the rice, and shape into a triangle. (Create two of these.)

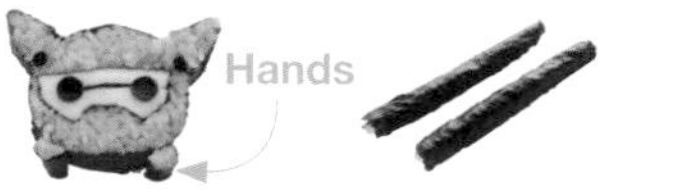
Hands

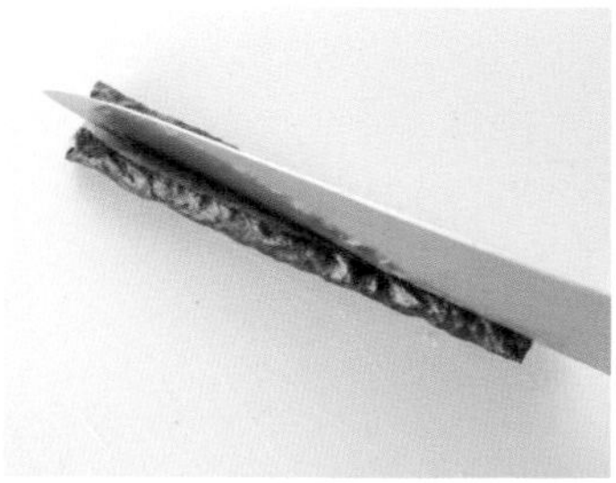

Place vinegared rice, 0.35 oz / 10 g, in a stick shape on the 1/8 nori sheet, roll and cut it lengthwise in half.

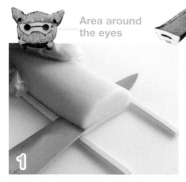

Area around the eyes

1 Cut the kamaboko fish cake leaving a slice of 5-6 mm / 0.2–0.24 inches on the board. You can also cut the entire fish cake off, and use chopsticks to slice off 5-6 mm / 0.2-0.24 inches evenly.

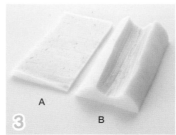

2 Create a slit along each side and cut into the shape of Baymax's eyes. (→ Refer to the sample image on p. 88)

3 What it looks like after slicing the top part off.

4 Fold a 1/8 nori sheet in half (→ See p. 88) and place in the center of A.

5 Put B on top of 4.

6 Wrap the whole thing with a 3/8 size nori sheet.

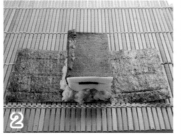

7 Shape and fill the indentation on the top.

Attention!

It is important to choose a kamaboko fish cake that is similar to the shape of the area around Baymax's eyes. Choose a fish cake that isn't too tall and gently rounded on the top.

2. Assemble and Roll

1 Place the sushi mat sideways on the table. Place a 1/2 size nori sheet on the mat and spread 1.8 oz / 50 g of vinegared rice 2 inches / 5 cm wide in the middle of the nori.

2 Place the eye area on the rice with the indentation facing down.

3 Cover it with 3.2 oz / 90 g of rice and shape it into a dome shape so the entire roll becomes an oval.

 does not

4 Keep the sushi mat on the table and wrap the nori around the roll by flipping each side of the sushi mat over.

3. Cutting and Finishing Touches

1 Adjust the shape of the roll, pat the sides to flatten and cut it into four equal slices.

2 Cut each of the horns and hands into four equal pieces and attach onto the face.

3 Hide the nori beneath the horn using the rice to erase the borderline.

4 Place the eyes on the end of the black line and add the decorations at the bottom of the horns.

Perry the Platypus

DIFFICULTY 1

Perry can be recognized by his large flat beak and three strands of hair. Place the glint inside his eye to add more expression.

actual size

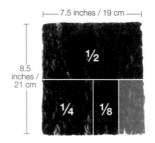

INGREDIENTS FOR FOUR SLICES

Vinegared Rice

Vinegared Rice (Blue), 7.76 oz / 220 g
(Vinegared rice 7.4 oz / 210 g + Deco Furi (sky) 0.35 oz / 10 g)

Ingredients

American cheese, 1 slice (beak, eyes)
Kelp cooked in sweet soy sauce, 1 slice (eyes)

Nori Sheets

⊢— 7.5 inches / 19 cm —⊣

8.5 inches / 21 cm

½

¼   ⅛

PREPARATION

Separate the vinegared rice into the various needed portions.

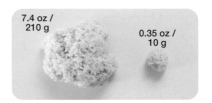

7.4 oz / 210 g

0.35 oz / 10 g

Cut the beak out of the cheese using a bamboo skewer and use a straw to punch the eyes out.

Eyes 8 ovals using a straw (wide)

Beak 4 sets

Eyes 8 circles using a straw (medium)

Squeeze the straw slightly to punch out the pupils from the soy sauce kelp and place small fragments of rice on them.

1. Creating the body parts

 Three strands of Hair

Stretch rice over the 1/4 size nori sheet as glue but leave the top and bottom 0.4 inch / 1 cm open.

Fold the center of the nori sheet into a mountain fold that is 0.6 inch / 1.5 cm tall.

Fold the remaining sides into 0.4 inch / 1 cm tall mountain folds too to create three strands of hair.

Hands

Place vinegared rice (white), 0.35 oz / 10 g, in a stick shape on the 1/8 nori sheet, roll and cut it lengthwise in half.

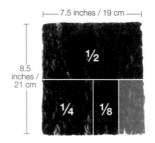

2. Assemble and Roll

Place the sushi mat upright on the table. Place 7.4 oz / 210 g of vinegared rice in a stick shape, on the nori leaving 1.2 inches / 3 cm open from the bottom.

Lift the bottom of the sushi mat while holding the vinegared rice and roll to the far end of the sushi mat.

3. Cutting and Finishing Touches

Adjust the shape of the roll, pat the sides to flatten and cut the roll into four equal slices.

Cut the each of the hands and the three strands of hair into four pieces. Attach the hands.

Place the beak and whites of the eyes onto the face and add the pupils on top.

Affix the three strands of hair firmly onto the roll by spreading rice as glue.

Sushi Cookbook

VIZ MEDIA EDITION

Author: Emi Tsuneoka

CREDITS – VIZ MEDIA
Translator: Tetsuichiro Miyaki
Recipe Testing: Emi Louie-Nishikawa
Design: Alice Lewis, Kam Li
Editor: Joel Enos

Printed in Malaysia

Published by VIZ Media, LLC
P.O. Box 77010
San Francisco, CA 94107

10 9 8 7 6 5 4 3 2 1
First Printing, September 2020

Library of Congress Cataloging-in-Publication data available.

CREDITS – JAPANESE STAFF

Editing: Mieko Baba

Photography: Mari Harada

Book Design: Natsuko Nagauchi, Yoshie Fujishiro, Takeshi Shibuya (JV Communications)

Cooperation:

Daimatsu Foods Co., Ltd. http://www.daimatsu-net.co.jp/

Japan Deco Sushi Association http://deco-sushi.com

Nico-Nico Nori Inc. http://www.niconico-nori.co.jp/

Hagoromo Foods Corporation http://www.hagoromofoods.co.jp/

Editor-in-Chief: Noriaki Sakabe

Issuer: Akira Naito

Publisher: Boutique-sha, Inc.

AUTHOR

Emi Tsuneoka

Japan Deco Sushi Association Curriculum Committee President
Lifestyle Information Website All About Deco Sushi Guide

Emi Tsuneoka made her debut as a sushi roll instructor in 2008. She has been teaching sushi roll art all over Japan at numerous nationwide classes, as well as appearing on TV shows and other online media. She has also presented many works with decorative cookies, decorative cupcakes, decorative accessories and decorative craftworks. She is also the author of *Fun to Make! Good to Eat!! Sushi Roll*.

BLOG	http://ameblo.jp/nandemodekiru/
WEBSITE	http://www.manoclasse-emi.com/
E-MAIL	info@manoclasse-emi.com

STAFF

Midori Motoki

BLOG
http://maitemiyou.jugem.jp/

E-MAIL
hanamakiko1219@gmail.com

Yukari Tanaka

WEBSITE
https://xn--w8jm3fycxc.com/

E-MAIL
nacaco-kinngyo@tau.e-catve.ne.jp

Mariko Uga

BLOG
https://www.uzumakiko.jp/

E-MAIL
uzumakiko55@gmail.com